Sicily: Island of Myths

Legas
Sicilian Studies
Volume XX
Series Editor: Gaetano Cipolla

Other Volumes Published in this Series:

1. Giuseppe Quatriglio, *A Thousand Years in Sicily: from the Arabs to the Bourbons*, transl. by Justin Vitiello, 1992, 1997;
2. Henry Barbera, *Medieval Sicily: the First Absolute State*, 1994, 2000;
3. Connie Mandracchia DeCaro, *Sicily, the Trampled Paradise, Revisited*, 1998; 2008;
4. Justin Vitiello, *Labyrinths and Volcanoes: Windings Through Sicily*, 1999;
5. Ben Morreale, *Sicily: The Hallowed Land*, 2000;
6. Joseph Privitera, *The Sicilians*, 2001;
7. Franco Nicastro and Romolo Menighetti, *History of Autonomous Sicily*, transl. by Gaetano Cipolla, 2002;
8. Maria Rosa Cutrufelli, *The Woman Outlaw*, transl. by Angela M. Jeannet, 2004;
9. Enzo Lauretta, *The Narrow Beach*, transl. by Giuliana Sanguinetti Katz and Anne Urbancic, 2004;
10. Venera Fazio and Delia De Santis, ed. *Sweet Lemons: Writings with a Sicilian Accent*, 2004;
11. *The Story of Sicily*, 2005. (Never printed);
12. Gaetano Cipolla, *Siciliana: Studies on the Sicilian Ethos*, 2005;
13. Paolo Fiorentino, *Sicily Through Symbolism and Myth*, 2006;
14. Giacomo Pilati, *Sicilian Women*, transl. by Anthony Fragola, 2008;
15. *Prayers and Devotional Songs of Sicily*, ed. & transl. by Peppino Ruggeri. 2009.
16. Giovanna Summerfield & John Shelly Summerfield, Jr. *Remembering Sicily*, 2009.
17. Joseph Cacibauda, *Ater Laughing Comes Crying: Sicilian Immigartns on Louisiana Plantations*, 2009;
18. Domenico Tempio, *Poems and Fables*, transl by G. Summerfield, 2010.
19. *Sweet Lemons 2: International Writings with a Sicilian Accent*, ed. by V. Fazio and D. DeSantis, 2010.

Giuseppe Quatriglio

Sicily:
Island of Myths

Translated

by

Florence Russo and Gaetano Cipolla

© Copyright Legas 2011

No part of this book may be translated or reproduced in any form, by print, photoprint, microfilm, microfiche, or any other means, without the written permission from the copyright holder.

Library of Congress Cataloging-in-Publication Data

Quatriglio, Giuseppe.
 [Isola dei miti. English]
 Sicily : island of myths / Giuseppe Quatriglio ; translated by Florence Russo and Gaetano Cipolla.
   p. cm. -- (Sicilian studies ; v. 20)
   ISBN 1-881901-78-5 (pbk. : alk. paper) 1. Sicily (Italy)--Social life and customs. 2. Sicily (Italy)--Biography. 3. Legends--Italy--Sicily. 4. Popular culture--Italy--Sicily. 5. Sicily (Italy)--History, Local. 6. Historic sites--Italy--Sicily. I. Russo, Florence, 1966- II. Cipolla, Gaetano, 1937- III. Title. IV. Title: Island of myths.
 DG865.6.Q82 2011
 945'.8--dc22

2010054428

This book was originally published in 2009 by Flaccovio Editore, Palermo, with the title *L'isola dei miti*.

Acknowledgements

The publisher gratefully acknowledges Mr. Anthony J. Miele's generous grant, made in memory of his beloved wife Frances Pisano, that in part made the publication of this book possible.

Preliminary versions of a few chapters in this book were done as projects in Prof. Cipolla's course on Literary Translation by the following students: Melissa Bondi, Catherine Di Giovanni, Alba Dominguez, Patrick Duffy, Simona Perego, Francesco Pizzolla and Susana Vasquez.

For information and for orders, write to:

Legas

P.O. Box 149
Mineola, NewYork
11501, USA

3 Wood Aster Bay
Ottawa, Ontario
K2R 1D3 Canada

legaspublishing.com

Table of Contents

Preface 7

Palermo in the Age of the Florios 9

The Queen of Palermo 13

Wagner and the Hotel delle Palme 17

Palermo's Mountain 24

Frederick II's Falcons 28

The Zisa and the Devils 32

Roger II in Vienna 36

Charles V in Sicily 41

Cagliostro, Palermitan and Cosmopolitan 47

A Magician in Cefalù 52

The Irony of the Catanesi 57

The Allure of Etna 61

The Eco of Bellini's Melodies 66

A Refuge for Giovanni Verga 71

The Legend of "Nick the Fish" 76

The Marsala Adventure 82

Ulysses in Sicily 85

The Trinacria in England 90

The Vacation Island.. 94

In Pirandello's Homes 98

A Hotel Symbol.. 104

Sciascia: a Destiny 108

Preface

According to Niccolò Tommaseo's *Dizionario della lingua italiana,* the word "myth" can identify also "a thing or a person about whom everyone is talking."

This definition encouraged me as I was pondering the title for this book. In fact, I have put together essays relating to entities, persons and circumstances that can be found in everyday conversations, arousing curiosities that often are not satisfied. It is, therefore, not a journey to the realm of classical mythology and the Olympus created by the ancients' imagination, but rather a reconnoitering of the heritage of popular truths and impressions that are part of our daily lives, raising questions that often demand our attention.

Isn't the complex story of a large entrepreneurial family, lived with daring, luxury and waste, at the center of which there stood the figure of a *femme fatale,* Franca Florio, a matter of myth? Aren't fabulous stories still told about the Emperor Frederick II—crowned king when he was four years old in the Palermo Cathedral—and about his trained falcons? Isn't the historical event of Charles V's month-long stay in Palermo shrouded in mystery? The Emperor, according to a sly chronicler, was certainly more cautious than he was chaste. How can one forget Wagner in Palermo and the cult of the great composer that has never waned in the hotel that welcomed him as a guest? What about the devils in the Zisa palace? Do they not keep dancing before our eyes, jumping around in the vast painting in the Norman-era palace in a way that you cannot count them?

Don't we still try to find the home where the worldly traveler Balsamo-Cagliostro was born, who from a small street in the Ballarò section ended up in the heart of Europe? How can one forget A. Crowley, the perverse English magician who settled down with his court of concubines in Cefalù during the Fascist era? Don't we still recall the legendary passing of Ulysses in the Trinacria of primordial times? And isn't the colorful fable of Colapesce still fascinating?

Isn't the highest volcano in Europe a representation of the mountain *par excellence* and isn't Mount Pellegrino, the mountain that fascinated Goethe, whose massive presence in the landscape of Palermo makes it invisible to the people who see it before their eyes every day? And wasn't the Marsala wine that Admiral Nelson ordered on board his ships so he could offer a nectar to his sailors during moments of rest a novelty on the table of the gourmands as well as a technological advance in Nineteenth century Sicily?

The fantastic tales are intertwined with reflections on the great men of the past, Bellini and Verga, and those closer to us, Pirandello and Sciascia.

These and many others are the topics presented in the chapters of this book. I hope they will evoke curiosity and interest, but above all I hope you will enjoy them.

Palermo in the Age of the Florios

"The new elegant sections, the new vast, tree-lined squares, the magnificent public walking areas—true delightful places worthy of Paris and London, did not alter the city's original ancient physiognomy that is still represented by two interminable straight avenues (Via Maqueda and Via Vittorio Emanuele) that intersect at the city center.

"...Judging by the traffic on those two avenues one would think that Palermo was a city of two million inhabitants. In both avenues from one end to the other there flows a wave of people, carts, coaches, and vehicles that continuously maneuver to avoid hitting one another, that meet in a thousand points and get confused, they stop, they form massive traffic jams. The swarming of people and carts confuses the view, the cacophony stuns your brain, a variety of vehicles loaded with different objects, a variety of human faces, gestures, voices, a contrast between cheerfulness and fury, of hard work and play, of luxury and poverty the likes of which you cannot find in any other city in the world."

This characterization written by Edmondo De Amicis in a book published after a voyage to Sicily in 1906, records colorful, but realistic images of Palermo. The city at the foot of Mt. Pellegrino, laid out guarding the Golden Conch, lived in those days —even in the face of strident social differences—a season open to hope and the seduction of progress from 1891 and 1892 when it welcomed the vast National Exposition situated on one hundred thirty thousand square meters of space in the new section of town. That exposition of the industrial and commercial capabilities of Italy was in tune with other analogous initiatives in the country, but in Palermo it functioned as a wake up call. It intensified the desire to do things and accelerated the modernization of urban structures. Oresto Lo Valvo underlined this when he wrote in the *Ultimo Ottocento palermitano* that from the National Exposition the city had changed its "face and soul." From 1899 the first steel-grinding electric trams were circulating along the city streets shaving replaced the two-horse-drawn busses. But the new century, in reality, brought about a definite change in the realm of floral designs in Europe. It was a fantastic style flowing with allegorical figures represented by the works of Ernesto Basile and Ettore De Maria Bergler.

The photographic album of Palermitan life at the time records emblematic images, especially the parade of shining, private coaches along the Viale della Libertà, still not lined with trees, and the ample lanes of the Marina, in a competition of luxury and worldly sophistication. The parades were reminders of the pomp displayed by wealthy ladies of high society at theatrical events, sumptuous receptions in the worldly rituals of the most exclusive clubs. In those days, the doors to their splendid palaces were not opened simply by the princes and dukes, not only by the Mazzarinos, the Niscemis, the Lanzas of Scalea and the Lanzas of Trabia, but also by the representatives of a new entrepreneurial elite, with the Florios and the Whitakers in first place. The third largest lyrical theater in Europe, after the ones in Paris and Vienna, had been inaugurated in 1897 with Verdi's *Falstaff* with Enrico Caruso. Six years after that, in 1903, the businessman Andrea Biondo, together with his brother and later his wife Margherita, opened a new prose theater with a show starring Ermete Novelli. Andrea Biondo's act was pure philanthropy because he built the theater on Via Roma, out of his love for the stage, without public financing. With the Politeama Theater already open and with other smaller theatrical venues, Palermo offered quality entertainment.

Liberty was the predominant architectural style. That was the style of grand little villa belonging to the Florios, that was the style used to build Villa Igiea, which was transformed by the Florio family from a sanatorium into a luxury hotel. That was the style of many other buildings along the urban axis that the blind mattocks of reconstruction inexorably erased later. *La Belle Epoque* imposed its own liturgies. The new wealthy and the titled nobility, just as they did in Milan or Rome, followed the British fashions and bought their expensive clothing directly in London. And in the name of emancipation, the ladies of high society—with their narrow waistline and skirts down to their ankles—went to the center of town by themselves to shop. The men were the main players in the coffee shops. They spent long hours moving about in padded living rooms, enveloped by the smoke and smell of cigars and by the rustling of much sought-after *cocottes*. The men had other interests: an overwhelming passion for the Targa Florio car race and speedy automobiles: a mania for duels when an offense had to be washed off in blood, even if it consisted of a minor scratch.

Yet Palermo at that time held an intellectual primacy. It was represented by the activities of the Mathematical Club, which regularly sent authoritative summaries of its research to scientific institutions around the world. Even the artisan trade was flourishing on account of the orders received that kept expert ironworkers, carpenters, decorators, and builders of coaches occupied. Out of that sparkling society at the beginning of the century rose the star of Franca Florio.

Advertising in newspapers, which was called "reclame" those days, offered the most genuine image of the tastes of the epoch. In the letters to the newspapers you could read hopeless messages of love like the following: "Don't you hear my desperate screams? I adore you in spite of everything. Fatal woman, I am yours, dead or alive." But the newspaper advertising carried also the echoes of courageous though doomed-to-fail entrepreneurial initiatives. One of these was offered by the four cylinder APIS automobile, entirely built in Palermo. In the first decade of the twentieth century, Palermo had the luster of a capital city. The golden chronicles of those years recorded the presence of a Rothschild and a Vanderbilt, but also of the King of Siam with an unpronounceable name, of Theodore Roosevelt ho came to the island in 1908 after leaving the Presidency in the hands of William Howard Taft. Those were the years when Edward VII, King of England who stayed in Palermo with his Queen Alexandra, and of William II, the German Kaiser. The sepia-tone photograph portray them in the Florio estate at the Olivuzza or in the park of Villa Malfitano in front of the solid residence built in the green space of via Dante by Joseph Whitaker, the wine industrialist who discovered the island of Motya. The masters of color Francesco Lojacono, Michele Catti, and Michele Cortegiani, as well as many other painters of their school, captured light on the marinas that smelled of algae and on sleepy hamlets, on nearby mountains and on the avenue flanked with plane trees. These fascinating images were linked to others such as those from fashion shows, of pastry and coffee shops always brimming with beautiful people that made news. The chronicles of social life talked about memorable parties, costume parades with the participation of high nobility scions, exhibiting their jewels and precious necklaces. The joy of living was a shining, little mirror that hid the squalor of the poor peoples' quarters with its social and urban degradation.

In the Kalsa quarter, hundreds of barefoot and malnourished children were gathered by father Giovanni Messina, a courageous priest who had managed to raise a hospice with his own hands at the edge of the elegant walking area of the Marina. There, in what was at the beginning a hut, the priest waited for charity so he could feed his hungry children.

The first shock wave hit the city in 1909 when numerous wounded survivors of the disastrous Messina and Reggio Calabria earthquake arrived there. The following year, everything seemed forgotten when an enormous crowd filled piazza Pretoria to listen to Gabriele D'Annunzio who came to celebrate the fiftieth anniversary of Garibaldi's enterprise. There followed a host of parties, brilliant concerts, horseback hunts, but the lights that illuminated the Palermo stage were destined to be extinguished soon.

The world of labor was shaken with strikes, the national political climate changed. In 1911, the war to conquer Libya broke out, causing people to open their eyes to reality. Palermitans saw many ships leave from their ports carrying soldiers in colonial uniform. The fourth shore was represented by the predominant rhetoric as the "promised land," in spite of the warnings by Gaetano Salvemini. It finally was revealed that the enterprise was nothing more than a *big box of sand*, full of traps.

The noise of war, which was to last through the entire period of the Great War, covered the follies, the hopes, and the illusions of the *Belle Epoque*.

The Queen of Palermo

Franca Florio, Ignazio Florio's very beautiful wife, was born in Palermo in 1873. She was the only daughter of Baron Pietro Jacona of San Giuliano and Costanza Notarbartolo of Villarosa. She was emblematic of Sicilian beauty: she was very appealing though a bit stark on account of her olive complexion and her black hair which framed a perfectly oval face. That's how Ignazio Florio Jr. saw her for the first time as an adolescent, walking on a path in Villa Giulia accompanied by her nanny and her cousins, Francesca and Emma Villarosa. He was a young entrepreneur, heir to a substantial fortune. As he later stated, Ignazio was struck by her dark green eyes and her jet black hair.

At that time, young ladies were supposed to have light and rosy complexions like peaches and Franca was a rare sight in the panorama of Sicilian beauties. Nevertheless, as soon as she had the opportunity, young Franca had the color of her face lightened in Paris, arousing her husband's anger who evidently preferred her darker complexion. Franca had literally undergone torture in a beauty institute of the French capital where they had stripped her facial skin in pieces substituting a liquid patina.

Her married life was not fortunate. She married Ignazio in February 1893, when she was twenty years old, in spite of the reservations her father had on the young Florio scion whom he regarded as too fond of travels, enjoyment and beautiful women. But her husband proved to be affectionate and above all in love with her.

Franca Florio.

After nine months, their first daughter, Giovannuzza, was born, but she died at a very young age. The second born, a son whom they named Ignazio, but called Baby Boy, died very young, too, causing despair and unhappiness to their parents who lost the longed-for heir. In spite of these mournful events, Franca and Ignazio Florio continued to live in the golden ambiance that their rank in society demanded. In their Palermo residence in the Olivuzza section, which was like a royal palace, the couple organized parties that have remained memorable: they received princes and reigning kings among whom the German Kaiser William II with the Empress Augusta Victoria and Edward VII of England. But in that house they also organized a "kitchen for the poor," which prepared meals for many have-nots on a daily basis.

As a woman with a regal posture, Franca served as Lady in Waiting for Queen Elena from 1901 onward. Franca Florio wore fabulous jewelry which cost several million Lire at the time. Among them there was a diamond collier identical with the one owned by Queen Alexandra, the wife of the English King. She was treated like a reigning monarch, and indeed in Italy and outside the national boundaries, she was known as "the Queen of Palermo."

She was admired by monarchs and by famous artists. Gabriele D'Annunzio was infatuated with her and sent her every new novel he wrote with a dedication; painters Giovanni Boldini and Francesco Paolo Michetti painted her as a *femme fatale*; the sculptor Pietro Canonica signed his name on her marble bust together with the princess Doria Pamphili; Ruggero Leoncavallo compared her to the poetess Vittoria Colonna, immortalized by Michelangelo. Nevertheless, in December 1908, on hearing of the disastrous Messina earthquake, Franca Florio who was in her fifth month of pregnancy sailed to the bay of the destroyed city on their yacht *Sultana*, loaded with medicine, food, and clothing. Ignazio joined the crews who were digging among the rubbles trying to free people screaming for help. On board Franca gave proof of her willingness to help by preparing warm meals and taking care of the wounded who had been brought on the boat. Afterwards, during the Great War, she volunteered as a Red Cross nurse in the Palermo hospital, as did other young women of high society.

In the 1920s, Ignazio and his family's fortune began to decline after a rise that had been constantly favored by government men through various periods. Nevertheless, in 1925, Franca Florio hosted George V of England and Queen Mary at her Villa Igiea residence. Ten years after that the family's situation was disastrous. A letter sent to her by Ignazio in 1934 from a small hotel in Milan is telling. He revealed to his wife that he had to pawn this tie pin in order to get some cash. Almost certainly the tie pin was made of gold with precious stones on it.

In 1922, Franca Florio was robbed of the jewels that she had carelessly left in her hotel room. Among them there was a string of 360 pearls that was worth two million lire. She was lucky to get them back after the police arrested the international thieves who had not yet disposed of the jewel. But shortly after that, her husband was forced to give them to his creditors.

She died in 1950 at 77 years of age, seven years before Ignazio. She had lost her hearing and had no more illusions. Luck had definitely turned away from the Florios and their immense fortune was squandered.

At the end of 1939, as Orazio Cancila wrote, the liquidation of the Florio Financial Institution cost IRI almost 30 million lire. "It was a substantial loss for the Italian State that burdened itself with the impossible task of trying to save the Florio House."

The parabola of this southern entrepreneurial family known all over Europe seems to be unique in recent Italian history. It was a commanding show of courage, daring acts, gambles and bets, framed in the heart of the *Belle Epoque* whose fatuous world was made of empty sparkle. The last Florios lived through the leisure and splendors of the Liberty style represented by Basile and Ettore De Maria Bergler.

The first Florios had come to Sicily from Calabria at the turn of the Nineteenth century. In a popular section of Palermo, with managerial skills rare for the times, they had operated a drugstore, or as they called it then, a store for the sale of drugs and colonial merchandise. A century later, the last members of the family were involved in numerous enterprises, probably too many, which went from tuna fishing on the island of Favignana to the production of Marsala wine, to banking and shipping.

Their lives followed a novelistic model, if you consider hat Franca Florio, "The Queen of Palermo," found herself at the center of the international social scene. During the fortunate years, she and her husband took part in cruises, spent long vacations in the famous health spas, constantly flaunting their wealth. Faithful to her role, Franca devoted herself to helping the poor and getting involved in social assistance work. But this activity did not prevent her from sitting down at the gambling tables of half Europe, dilapidating enormous sums of money, even when her husband's fortune had inexorably begun to decline. She did this with fatalism and lack of conscience, even if, as she repeated, it was to distract her from her family's misfortunes.

Her story thus was completed between history and myth which the French historian Maurice Aymard compared to the story of the Buddenbrook family, the main characters of the Thomas Mann novel.

Wagner and the Hotel delle Palme

Richard Wagner and the Hotel delle Palme represent two names that the people of Palermo who are fond of historical memories often associate. The reason for this is that between 1881 and 1882, for four and a half months, the great German composer at the peak of his career lived in the hotel. Palermo was living in the luster years of the *Belle Epoque* era and Wagner marked the highest point of the Palermitan season among the nobility and the entrepreneurial class that celebrated rituals of luxury and worldliness.

Richard Wagner, in a portrait by Renoir.

Wagner arrived in Palermo on November 5, 1881 and as soon as the ship, the Simeto, moored at the Four Winds pier, he went to the Hotel delle Palme in a carriage. His wife Cosima, the daughter of Franz Lizst, accompanied him. She had divorced the Maestro Hans Von Bulow. Their children, Sigfried, twelve years old then, and the younger daughters, Eva and Isolde, were with the couple, as well as the young Blandina and Daniela, Cosima's daughters from her previous marriage. Part of the group were the Russian painter Paul de Joukowski, a set and costume designer who eventually designed the set for *Parsifal*, Sigfried's private tutor and two servants. A friend of the composer was already in Palermo: the pianist Joseph Rubinstein who had suggested to Wagner to choose the Grand Hotel des Palmes because among the great hotels in the city it offered its guests access to a luxuriant park containing many tropical plants and a winter garden.

The building had belonged to the English merchant Benjamin Ingham who sold it in 1874 for twenty thousand *scudi* to the young Enrico Ragusa, son of Salvatore Ragusa, the savvy owner of the Hotel Trinacria. When Wagner arrived, the hotel had been in business for only four years, but already Ingham's residence had undergone many changes. They had added a third floor and the entrance, which was originally on via Stabile, was opened facing the sea on what was to become via Roma.

Wagner occupied a luxurious suite on the second floor comprising three bedrooms and a hall that the maestro used as a studio. It was certainly the best of all the apartments he had had during his year-long stay in Naples, Amalfi and the Villa Rufolo in Ravello, whose garden he visualized as the ideal garden for the magician Klingsor, the main character of the opera *Parsifal* that he expected to complete in Palermo. But when he arrived there, he was nervous and alarmed by a persistent pain in his chest and a pimple in his face. Nevertheless, when he opened the balcony of the new apartment, the mild air heartened him and made him exclaim: "Here there is only spring and summer."

Born in Leipsig in 1813, Wagner was sixty eight years old in 1881. He had had an adventurous past. He had written and presented a number of operas, revisiting the old myths of his land and giving new life to literary and poetic themes of the German tradition, the sagas of German mythological heroes, the Nibelungen. His fantastic visions were accompanied by a music that had a symphonic, nervous and sometimes sensual character which was to delight Hitler and his entourage.

Wagner had been fascinated by the legend of the Phantom Ship and by the German folk songs elaborated during the Romantic age which recalled the story of the knight seduced by Venus; he had felt tenderness for the story of Lohengrin and his swan, he had paused with his music on the *Meister Singers* of Nuremberg, on the myths of the Rhinegold and *Walkiries*, on the *Twilight of the Gods*, and on the idyl of *Sigfried*, accompanied by a cosmic vision of sound.

The idea of *Parsifal* had been in his head for over forty years from the time he lived in Paris, but many vicissitudes had crossed his life.

The composer who in 1881 was a hero kissed by fame, had suffered through days of hunger in Paris and had been forced to adapt and even transcribe pieces for local bands to make a living. He even had to rely on pawn shops. He had also been a revolutionary in Dresden together with Bakunin and had risked getting arrested. Always besieged by debts, he had asked for loans from his friends, but his music had enchanted the nineteen year old Ludwig II of Bavaria. The young King had welcomed him as a god and allowed him to live at Villa Triebscen on Lake Lucerne with Cosima. He had even made it possible for him to build his own theatre in Bayreuth, giving him a grant of three thousand florins.

A lover of beautiful women, he had had many of them. As a husband, he had not always been faithful. But he had been betrayed by his first wife, Minna Pinter, who died in 1866. Only during his mature years, when he achieved world fame, did Wagner behave like a patriarch.

When he arrived in Palermo, he was at the apex of his glory and in spite of the numerous health problems, he felt he had a great deal of energy. In fact, he exclaimed once: "Is it true that I am sixty-eight years old? It seems impossible to me." But crabby as he was, he made French painter Pierre-Auguste Renoir who had come to Palermo to paint his portrait, wait for a long time. He finally received the painter in December 1882 and gave him half an hour of his time. Renoir related that they had exchanged a few words in French and in German and that Wagner after twenty minutes became impatient and stiffened. The painter said that if he had given him more time than the thirty five minutes he granted him his painting would have come out better. When the maestro glanced at the sketch and saw himself painted like a grand old man wrapped in a dark velvet jacket, he apparently exclaimed: "I look like a Protestant pastor." And the painter could do nothing else but nod. Today that painting hangs in a Paris museum.

The first weeks of the extended Wagner family's sojourn passed in absolute quiet as the composer tried to recapture the spirit of his work. His wife Cosima who kept a diary of their activities wrote: "We work in the morning, at midday we take a walk, we eat at one 'clock, at three in the afternoon we walk again, at five o'clock we work, at seven we dine and after that we go to bed." In reality, there was also time for reading and their favorite books were German classics, Kant and Goethe.

The program did not have many variants and Wagner managed to keep it until he and his wife were sucked in by the worldly Palermitan social scene, also on account of Blandina and Daniela who were two beautiful and blond young women who attracted the admiration of the aristocratic scions ready to do anything to have them as guests at their parties and receptions in their gilded palaces.

The Tascas, the Lanzas, the Gancis, the Mazzarinos and even the Florios made contact with the illustrious guests of the city and vied to invite them. A chronicler noted that every day no less than three blazoned carriages brought noblemen to the hotel to meet with Wagner.

People started gossiping. Tina Whitaker, the wife of the discoverer of ancient Motya, wrote in her diary: "He is arrogant and imperious and his total lack of sensitivity for the feelings of others was particularly bothersome to me. The relationship was made ever more tense by the exaggerated personality cult that Lady Cosima encouraged. I remember that one day when we went to visit him at the Hotel, the maestro suddenly stopped talking as though he were in a trance. Lady Cosima quickly came to whisper in our ears in French: 'I think the maestro is about to have a moment of inspiration. For this reason, we should end our conversation now.' We hurried out of there on tiptoes without even saying good-bye. Rachele Varvaro, who lived across the street from the Hotel, explained what happened whenever inspiration came to him. According to the type of inspiration, they threw a veil on the head of the maestro of different colors so that his visions would be colored by those hues."

When the Wagner family came to know the city, the composer who had been an untiring walker in his youth, devoted himself to long walks. He visited the cathedral and stood in reverent silence before the tomb of Frederick II; he admired the Palatine Chapel and the Monreale mosaics. He often went to the Foro Italico wearing a velvet cap, stopping once in a while to gaze at the sea before him. He went to Villa Giulia in a carriage. And when a Bavarian periodical wrote that the great musician's solitary walks exposed him to the risk of being held for ransom that the Italian Government would have had to pay, a local paper was outraged as Wagner himself who uttered a poisonous remark: "The only brigand that I have met here is Ragusa, the owner of my hotel." Ragusa had handed the German composer, who expected to be treated as a special guest, a very stiff bill.

Wagner's group was drawn in the worldly social life of Palermo's aristocracy. And that is how Cosima's daughter, Blandina von Bulow, met the young count Biagio Gravina, son of the Prince of Rammacca, an officer in the Italian Navy. He asked her to marry him and Count Tasca made the official request during a private conversation with the Wagner couple. Cosima was pleased and they accepted the offer.

The Trabia, Ganci and Tasca families opened their living rooms to the illustrious Germans. They even went as far as asking them to live in their residences. Wagner, however, was particularly interested in finishing the orchestrations for *Parsifal*. That happened on January 13, 1882, a date that the Maestro celebrated together with his family. While the family celebrated the birthday of their painter friend, Joukowsky, Wagner showed up and said to them: "I have completed my *Parsifal* for

The entrance of the Grand Hotel delle Palme in Palermo.

your birthday." They made a toast and for the occasion Wagner sat at the piano and played the ouverture of his opera *The Fairies*, written half a century before.

Parsifal, whose orchestration he had just completed, had been conceived as a sacred scenic action centered on the representation of the Holy Grail, an opera full of mysticism and pantheistic religious feelings that the author had lately embraced.

Once his most serious obligation was met, Wagner, who was concerned about the hotel expenses and as he could not have a rented villa all to himself, decided to accept the invitation of the Prince of Ganci. So on February 2, the whole family moved to the Porrazzi, Ganci's summer residence. In that isolated location, however, it was very cold and Sigfried fell ill. But the head of the family obtained some heaters and things went better after that. Wagner felt as though he had been reborn and he had the pleasure of playing a harpsichord, kept there as a relic on which Vincenzo Bellini had played. Wagner was moved and played the overture from *Norma* in homage to the great Catanese composer.

Before leaving Palermo, in the Porrazzi villa, in the presence of members of ruling foreign families, Wagner conducted the municipal band. They played the *Kaisermarch* and the *Huldigundmarch*. Afterward, at the end of his Sicilian sojourn, to show his gratitude for the hospitality he had received, he wrote a piece that he entitled "Tempo di Porrazzi." He left it for the owners, together with the baton used for conducting the farewell concert.

On March 19, 1882, the large family left Palermo heading for Acireale. They went there to celebrate the betrothal of Blandina with Count Gravina Rammacca in their family residence. In Acireale, two famous old men who would soon disappear from the world scene failed to meet: Richard Wagner and Giuseppe Garibaldi.

The anecdotes about the event are uncertain, but it seems that the train carrying Garibaldi, unable to move because of his arthritis, stopped at the Acireale station where the crowd was cheering for him. The station was in front of the Hotel delle Terme where the Wagner family had arrived a few days before. Wagner was curious to learn who the man was for whom the crowd was cheering and the hotel employee told him that he was Garibaldi, the Hero of Two Worlds. If these two great men had met, it would have been a momentous event.

There was a great party at Rammacca palace and the modalities of the wedding between Blandina and Biagio were arranged. The wedding was celebrated that same year on August 25, in Bayreuth.

Once he reluctantly left Sicily, Wagner stayed in Naples and then in Venice. On July 26, in the composer's own theater at Bayreuth, the opera *Parsifal* was performed. The first performance of the opera in Palermo occurred only in 1914 when Gino Marinuzzi became the director of the Massimo Theater.

Wagner settled in the Vendramin Palace during his stay in the city of the lagoon. And it was there that on February 13, 1883, he passed away following a heart attack. The great composer, lying on a red sofa, breathed his last holding onto Cosima's hand who had come running on hearing the sound of the bell. Someone recorded his last words whispered at the final moment. "Meine uhr" which in German can mean " My hour" but also "My watch". Wagner could have meant that his final hour had arrived, or perhaps he was referring to his watch that had slipped onto the carpet. The widow who had been born in Bellagio in 1837, directed the maestro's theater with an iron hand. She died in 1930. She was over ninety.

In Palermo, the news of Wagner's death evoked deep sorrow in those who had known him. Sicilians discovered they were Wagnerians recalling the presence of the musical giant in their city.

A few years after, the French writer Guy de Maupassant, being in Palermo, asked to see the rooms where the German composer had lived and then described the emotion he felt on opening the musician's bedroom closet: "Immediately a delightful and sharp perfume emanated from it. The owner of the hotel told me that Wagner wanted his linens sprayed with the essence of roses. That perfume was still there."

Today the Hotel delle Palme, which was restructured and expanded in 1907 by the magician of the Liberty style, Ernesto Basile, is not the same as the hotel of the late nineteenth century, but Wagner's stay there is commemorated on a marble slab that says somewhat rhetorically that the Maestro "yearning for the Sicilian sky, completed here one of his immortal operas." In the center of the hall you can see a bronze bust of the musician, not signed by its sculptor, and the gold wooden stool he used when he sat at the piano. The rooms where the Wagners stayed have been transformed and the studio of the composer is now a vast hall—The Wagner Room—that has a sumptuously decorated ceiling and a great crystal chandelier.

The Hotel delle Palme, with its padded corridors, preserves the secrets of its long history. During the night between the 13 and 14 of July 1933, the French surrealist writer Raymond Roussel died mysteriously in one of its rooms. Ten years later, following the occupation of the city by the Allies, the American General Charles Poletti established his headquarters in the hotel and sent from there his encrypted messages. As soon as the Americans went away, the great hotel was the place for obscure meetings between representatives of the Sicilian mafia and their United States counterparts.

Many memories survive among those who cultivate history. Almost all of the high class tourists who frequent the five-star hotel know nothing about its long history that began in the latter part of the nineteenth century.

Palermo's Mountain

The most exalting appraisal on the mountain of Palermo was Goethe's who in 1787 defined it as: "The most beautiful promontory in the world." At that time, the mountain closed off the gulf with sharp and defined outlines and looked marvelous in its bareness. But even today, as we drive on the highway we suddenly find ourselves before the rocky giant that acts as background to the asphalt ribbon and looks like a floating island between sea and sky, almost like a mirage, an imaginary vision. Nevertheless, we are usually too wrapped up with other concerns to think about this extraordinary view and we let only those who see it for the first time marvel at the sight of Mount Pellegrino. These hurried observations may be used as the starting point to reclaim the importance of the values hidden inside this stone giant that stands guard over Palermo and to protect it from building speculations, preserving its environment and nature, as well as to begin a systematic research into her long history.

Mount Pellegrino is in reality a jewel box containing archeological, historical and religious treasures. Its irregular shape, deep caves, cliffs

A view of Mount Pellegrino from the water.

and steep drops provide evidence of the long work done by nature. Owing to its isolation and inaccessibility, the mountain was used for defense and offense, providing shelter to primitive men as we can see from the traces left in the caves. The presence of the Phoenicians and the Greeks is, however, better documented.

In 1917, during the construction of a roadway, workers found ceramic fragments of amphorae, vases, lanterns and tiles that were attributed to the Carthaginian settlement that stayed on the mountain for three years from 248 to 245 BC. We know that Asdrubal and Hamilcar Barca were able to withstand the attack of the Roman legions composed of forty thousand soldiers on horses. In the end, they had to give up and the Romans reached the high cliffs abandoned by their enemies. But they did not remain there for long, so that very little of that occupation remains, but the Greek and Phoenician coins found in different eras give tangible proof both of the military operations conducted there, as well as of the settlements that lasted longer.

Mount Pellegrino was abandoned both during the later Roman era and in the darkest days of the middle ages. In the sixteenth century, the northeastern flank of the mountain was used as a stone quarry for the expansion of the port of Palermo during the De Vega vice-regency. But for a long time Mount Pellegrino was used for hunting and grazing sheep, as well as a refuge for hermits.

Surrounded by a halo of legend, the large grotto on the top of the mountain welcomed in the Norman era the noblewoman Rosalia Sinisbaldi who moved there from the hills of Quisquina to live a solitary life according to the Benedictine rules. The courageous and lone Rosalia must have been helped by the other hermits and her body, after her passing, must have been hidden by them "in living rock", which was the custom for the Christians who had retired from the world to live in an exemplary manner.

According to the tradition, the body of Rosalia was found on July 15, 1624 by a hunter while the plague was devastating Palermo. The few bones mixed with rocks were finally recognized as belonging to the hermit on February 18 of the following year by a commission of doctors and theologians. Four days after, the remains were placed in a box and were brought to the Cathedral. The plague had passed, meanwhile, and the happy Palermitans did not want to wait until July 15 to celebrate the event. A little more than a month before that date, on June 9, the city decorated with triumphal arches, rich draperies hanging from windows, colored lanterns and jubilant signs, greeted the protector for the first time. That was the first pilgrimage, which initiated a long and continued tradition.

Immediately after that, the Senate decided to erect a sanctuary next to her grotto. The work started in a climate of exceptional fervor and was completed within three years. The inauguration occurred in the spring of 1624. At the same time, the virginal hermit of Mount Pellegrino was officially proclaimed a saint by Urban VIII. She became the patroness of the city, taking the place held by Saint Cristina.

The church that was built around the cave has always evoked a great deal of interest. The list of illustrious visitors is very long, but a reference to the already cited Goethe would suffice. On seeing the marble statue of the saint done by the Florentine Francesco Tudisco, Goethe was ecstatic. The great poet admired the golden dress that covered the statue which was worth two thousand *scudi* donated by Charles III in 1735, when he was crowned King in the Palermo Cathedral. Goethe never tired of admiring the "sleeping beauty" of the Saint and concluded his remarks with these words: "To make it short, I could not tear myself away from that place and I returned to Palermo only after dark."

A seventeenth century car for the feast of St. Rosalia.

Mount Pellegrino is not only the sacred mountain of the Palermitans, it is linked also to the great figure of Frederick II of Swabia. According to a legend with some historical truth behind it, the Emperor, having noticed that workers in the summer were forced to work beyond the required number of hours, ordered them to stop at sunset. To make everyone see when it was time to stop working, he ordered the placement of a large rock visible to all so that the mountain's shadow would fall on the rock at sunset. That was the time to stop working. It was known as the "Rock of the Emperor" and it remained in place until the first half of the eighteenth century. Mongitore testified to its existence in his *Sicilia Ricercata*.

Until the first decade of the twentieth century you could climb on Mount Pellegrino only through the wide flight of steps, the "Scala," built two hundred years before. The road was begun early in the new century, but was completed only in 1924 on account of the numerous interruptions for lack of funds and for the war. The original project intended to transform Mount Pellegrino into a climactic zone, allowing private people to buy lots to build residences. Fortunately, this project did not go forward. Only at the end of the 1920s, the Sicilian entrepreneur Michele Utveggio was allowed to build an edifice shaped like a medieval castle on a rocky projection facing Palermo. The inauguration occurred in 1931. Since then the temptations to build on the mountain have returned cyclically and some isolated authorizations have been given. Today, faced with ecological concerns, with the degradation of the urban and suburban areas, Mount Pellegrino represents the last frontier of the Palermitans, the last green oasis at the gates of the inhabited part, the park of the city *par excellence*.

Frederick II's Falcons

The peregrine falcon stands out in vivid colors from a precious illustrated manuscript kept in the Vatican Library, and bring us the image of a bird of prey with sharp eyes and proud demeanor who was a companion to emperors and noblemen in the long history of the Middle Ages. But the falcon is a sought-after bird even today when jet planes cross the sky. That is because the falcon is a bird of prey that can hunt seagulls and other birds that can be sucked in by jet engines and cause a plane to crash. The managements of many of the great airports around the world have engaged the services of many falconers and have bought whole nests of falcons, to remove this danger to planes.

The falcons, however, are not used only for utilitarian purposes, but also as a pastime, as was done in ancient times. In Italy, a falconers' club exists whose members hunt with the help of trained falcons. And in Geraci Siculo, a town in the Madonie mountains standing three thousand feet above sea level, you can see falcons fly out of the ruins of the Ventimiglia family castle from the gloved arm of one of the last descendants of the feudal family that possessed the fief in this mountainous area of Sicily. The flight of falcons pays homage to Frederick II and to his love for them and brings to mind the famous treatise written in Latin by the Emperor in his Palermo Royal Palace.

Frederick II and his falcon.

The treatise of the Swabian Monarch, *De arte venandi cum avibus (On the Art of Hunting with Birds)* has not lost its technical value, according to modern experts, even after so many centuries. That is certainly another accomplishment that can be added to the crown of Frederick II Hoenstaufen. The son of Henry VI, who on the day of the Pentecost in 1198, was crowned King of Sicily in Palermo at the age of four, was not only a political genius who understood the futility of fighting bloody crusades (so much so that he concluded one of them without blood letting, by signing an agreement with the Sultan of Egypt Al-Kamil) and a refined man who formed the "Sicilian School" that was regarded as the European center for poetry, but he was as well, among the great men of the Middle Ages, one of the most open to learning and science. With an enthusiasm that never waned, he dedicated himself to the study of mathematics, optics, astronomy, zoology, alchemy, medicine and hygiene. The historian Matteo Paris called him "Stupor mundi" (amazement of the world) for these reasons.

At his court in Palermo, Frederick II welcomed philosophers, artists, mathematicians, and learned men from every part of the world then known. He could address them in Latin, in *volgare* (the emerging Sicilian language) in French, German, Greek and Arabic: six languages he spoke fluently.

Michael Scotus, a renowned Scotsman who had the reputation of being an exceptional astrologer, was invited at court in 1227. Scotus had studied at Oxford and in Paris and had traveled to Spain to complete his education. In 1220, the Scotsman sent the Emperor the Latin translation of Avicenna's zoological treatise. This gift opened the door of Sicily for him. Seven years after that, Frederick named him official court astrologer.

Knowing something about Scotus' activities is important to learn about Frederick's scientific interests. In addition to translating Avicenna's treatise, Scotus prepared, on orders from Frederick II, an astrological compendium. He also wrote numerous medical and alchemical texts. He compiled a classification of the sciences, gathering his information from the mysterious veins of the culture of his time.

Michael Scotus' true personality began to shine at the Palermo court, in contact with that exceptional man who lived as an oriental prince, not dispensing with his harem, who had an undying desire and irresistible urge to see to the bottom of things.

Frederick II for some aspects remained a medieval spirit even though his intuitions went beyond the limits of this time. That is evident when we reread the "questions" that he asked learned men of this day, which today appear naïve and desperate for the unsatisfied desire for truth from which they originated. The Emperor wanted to know "the foundations of the earth, that is, how it stays still on top of the void." "In what heaven does God sit, how does he sit on the throne of the world?" "What do the Angels and the Saints do before God?" "Where are Hell, Purgatory and Paradise?" He asked also "how do the humors of the earth manage to give fruits their sweetness?" Also: "Why are there salt waters and fresh waters, hot springs and cold springs?" "What is the nature of the fire of Etna, Vulcano and Stromboli?"

Even when he went to the East, while the diplomatic negotiations were going on with the Sultan Al-Kamil for the cession of Jerusalem, he presented some questions on physics and astronomy, dictated by his insatiable scientific curiosity. He wanted to know, among other things, why objects that are partially immersed in water appear to be bent, what was the cause for the black little dots that at times jump before our eyes, and why the star Canopo appears to be bigger when it is closer to the horizon.

These questions notwithstanding, he astonished the Arabs for his competence in matters of medicine and human and animal anatomy. Frederick II was the founder of the first Chair in Anatomy at the Salerno School of Medicine, allowing students to study human bodies when autopsies were still forbidden as sacrilegious at the university of Bologna.

Just as King Roger had linked his name to a scientific work, the geography text compiled in collaboration with Edrisi, Frederick II is associated with a science treatise: the manual of the training of falcons to perform at man's bidding.

The treatise *De arte venandi cum avibus* displays not only a profound knowledge of every aspect of falconry, but includes an intelligent and systematic treatment of the different species and habits of the bird.

But whereas King Roger simply provided assistance to Edrisi in the writing of his geography treatise, Frederick II dictated the entire text and according to many scholars personally illustrated the codex that has come down to us. Undoubtedly, the work was born out of his passion for hunting, understood not "as a form of deceit or brute force bent to destroying the prey,"--as Antonino De Stefano put it—" but as an expression of physical vigor and perhaps more correctly as a spiritual exercise conducted with the collaboration of trained and intelligent animals." Hunting, for the Emperor was in the end a way of humbly studying nature. The laws passed by Frederick reflected this understanding. For the first time in history, hunting was regulated and the periods when hunting was forbidden were set in accordance with the reproductive cycles of birds.

He worked thirty years to complete his treatise. He summoned experts and technicians in the matter of falconry from Arabia, but he did not accept any information without putting it to the test personally. He collected falcons and similar birds of prey from England, from Asia Minor, and from India to compare them and to study their behavior. He accurately described their anatomical structures, their nesting habits, how to capture them and train them. He examined everything with an open and scientific mind.

He had already stated the possibility of artificially incubating chicken eggs. And he had turned his attention to horses, too. With economic, military, and scientific objectives in mind, he promoted a horse-breeding establishment in Puglia to cross-breed native horses with Arabian horses to improve the species.

In several localities of his Kingdom, he possessed animal parks where hunting was forbidden. In 1245, the monks of San Zeno in Verona had to arrange lodging for an elephant, five leopards and twenty-four camels, traveling with Frederick II. The presence of such a "serraglio" gives us a glimpse into Frederick's personality, his taste for magnificence and pomp on one side, but also his genuine interest in science, on the other.

It is surprising that a ruler whose life was besieged by excommunications, political intrigues, and wars, was able to devote so much time to study and pastime. In the preface to his work on falcons, he wrote: "Although we are entangled in the thorny and complex task of governing our realms and our empire, we have not abandoned our pursuits."

The German philosopher Nietzsche likened Frederick II to Leonardo da Vinci. And, in fact, there is something of da Vinci's in his eagerness to learn, in his desire to observe nature and penetrate its secrets. His contemporaries saw in Frederick's investigative nature, "the sign of pride and ungodliness." For this reason, Dante judged Frederick as a materialist and placed him among the Epicureans in hell. In truth, the Norman Royal Palace in Palermo was, thanks to this most enlightened of the Hoenstaufens, the only Chair from which—in the dark times of the Italian Middle Ages—you could cultivate the sciences of the visible world with remarkable freedom and without prejudices, and without running the risk of being condemned as a witch.

The Zisa and the Devils

The sight is similar to what you expect to see in an oriental fairy tale: a castle with a Muslim matrix mirrored in a fish pond 15 meters wide and 22 long. Beyond the pool, a ring of low bodies with fornices and then a green public park. In the center there is a fountain and beyond the park there is a square on the axis of a construction not lacking in surprises, if you think that it had a system of air circulation in all the rooms that was effective though rudimentary, and that it has fed ancient legends, like the one about devils guarding a treasure.

The Zisa Castle, standing alone in its imposing structure, is one of a kind in the Mediterranean area, and it has always fascinated people for

The Zisa Palace as it was at the turn of the twentieth century.

the memory of its ancient splendor. Consider the proud inscription on the ground floor that was translated from the Arabic by Michele Amari (author of the impressive *History of the Saracens in Sicily*): "As many times as you will want, you will see the most beautiful possession in the most splendid kingdom in the world... This is an earthly paradise that opens before your gaze, this is the *Mosta' izz* (yearning for glory) and this palace is the *Aziz* (the noble, the glorious)."

The building was begun by the Norman King of Sicily, William I, in the second half of the XII century and it was completed by his son William II (1154-1180), following the dominant Islamic art. The

Zisa—which is part of the Norman Royal park of Palermo that includes the Cuba, the castle of Favara and of Scibene—represents the most illustrious stone document of the Arab-Norman syncretism, that is, the continued use of the architectural ways of the Islamic world in an island dominated by conquerors who came form the north: a persistence due to the Muslim presence on the island that began in 827 and lasted a quarter of a millennium.

The Zisa's vicissitudes have been varied. The Norman chronicler Ugo Falcando praised it in the XII century. It was described by Leonardo Alberti, a monk from Bologna, in 1526. In 1440 the castle was given to Antonio Beccadelli by Alphonse of Aragon and in the following century Charles V gave it to Antonio de Faraone who had contributed with a donation of 5,000 florins to the Emperor's conquest of Tunis. In the Seventeenth century, during a plague, the castle became a deposit of illegal merchandise. It had been reduced to such poor conditions that it was given free to the buyer of the "land rights" of the Zisa. Only in 1951, following its acquisition by the Sicilian Region, did the monument start a new life. Nevertheless, it was only twenty years after, and following the collapse of one of its wings, that systematic and final restoration began under the direction of the architect Giuseppe Caronia.

Only then did the vastness of the damage become visible. The lack of consolidation following the expropriation, water infiltrations, vandals' theft of materials were the causes that opened up a gash 8 meters wide going from the ground floor to the ceiling. In addition heavy restructuring had been carried out in the course of centuries. Among them, the construction of a great internal staircase, completed by cutting through thick supporting walls.

The real work of restoration started in March 1974 with the constant concern to conciliate the static requirements with those of a historical and aesthetic nature. To this end, walls were plugged with bricks, ceilings and walkways were made lighter, baked bricks were recovered as well as ceramics and amphorae, (the latter had been inserted in the wall buttresses) that bore witness to the monument's long life. The restoration work required the elimination of tons of dead weight predominantly made of gravel. The architect Giuseppe Caronia in a book of the Zisa restoration related his coming to terms with the old stones.

Some interesting discoveries were made in the course of the eleven years spent in the restoration: they found layers of plaster painted in

A view of the flying devils on the ceiling of the Zisa palace.

white, red, and blue of Norman era, showing that the Norman rulers had painted the walls with vivid colors so that the building did not appear originally with naked stone as it does today. They did not find gold or silver coins and they did not find the legendary "truvatura," the treasure that many have sought for half a millennium, uselessly making holes in the old walls. What emerged was the exceptional unity of the Zisa's structure, a geometric harmony achieved though the symmetrical placement of each of its architectural elements. For the restorers, it was like coming across a key that had been buried for centuries, but which was still capable of opening a garden of marvels for the men of today. Boxed in internally with cement injections and with iron rods sealed with resin, the Zisa now can be seen with solid outside walls, elegant blind arches and the fountain hall with its oriental grace richly decorated with mosaics and with its alveoli ceiling.

Today the Zisa holds the first nucleus of the Museum of Islamic Civilization. In the rooms of the two floors devoted to the show (the fourth floor is still empty) there is a display of glazed ceramics, some of which bear inscriptions. The exhibition is composed of epigraphs, architectural elements, decorations and wooden structures. There are two rare Andalusian bronze mortars from the XI century and a little copper basin with scenes of hunting with a falcon from the following century. One of the points of attraction of the Zisa is the legend that was generated from the painted decoration whose date is unknown, above the high vault of the entrance arch. In this space that leads into the fountain hall, floating in the air within a wide oval area, you can see mythological figures.

The Zisa as it looks today after extensive restoration.

Popular culture has named them "devils" and identified them as the guardians of a treasure in gold coins hidden in the thick walls of the building. But the work of restoration, as we saw, has not revealed the existence of any treasures.

There are so many figures it is difficult to count them all. Looking at them from below, you have to raise your head and then turn to try to count them. But the count is always faulty because optical illusions lead people to commit errors.

The physician-ethnologist Giuseppe Pitrè observed that "the difficulty of counting the devils of the Zisa is due to the fact that some of the figures are very small and others not complete, so some people count them, others don't," an explanation that leaves you wondering.

In the course of the centuries, the optical illusion gave birth to the popular saying that interprets with a good dose of humor the painted figures as little, elusive, and devilish spirits. Hence, the devils of the Zisa.

Roger II in Vienna

There are many attractions in Vienna, the perennial symbol of the prestige of the old Hapsburg Empire. The city has that noble and reassuring look conferred to it by the solid baroque buildings, and the grandiose neoclassical, Nineteenth century constructions. Saint Steven, one of the best known Gothic churches in Europe, the immense Schonbrunn Palace in whose rooms the Restoration Congress of 1814 took place, the solemn Ring and the gay Prater, are must-see sights for those who come to the Austrian capital, but there is a corner of Vienna that a Sicilian cannot absolutely neglect because right in that place one of the living witnesses of distant historical events of the island is kept. I am referring to the "Schatzkammer," the room of the Imperial Treasure, and the witness is represented by the famous mantle of Roger II, made in Palermo in 1134, and by other precious heirlooms: the dalmatic, that is, the little tunic, the dawn of William II, the ceremonial gloves, the shin guards, the shoes of the Coronation, and the belt for the sword of Saint Mauritius.

The ever numerous public crowds the very rich museum guarded by many attentive custodians and are dazzled by the gold and sapphires of the Austrian imperial crown, a work of art by the Flemish goldsmith Vermeyen, they stop to admire the display windows with the imperial crown and globe, splendid symbols of the Holy Roman Empire used for crowning the emperors from the Middle Ages until the end of the eighteenth century, but when they reach the room that holds the coronation mantle of the Norman King of Sicily, Roger II, they gasp.

To the left, inside an enormous display cabinet, like an eagle with outstretched wings, you can see the famous mantle, a resplendent silk semicircle, decorated with gold and precious gems similar to a pluvial whose diameter is over three meters.

You cannot take pictures, not even of the people bending down to see the lower part of the mantle. The opportunity to capture an image that has emblematic value is lost and all one can do is ask the nearest custodian what the most admired pieces of the museum are. The answer is a compensation for the missed photo. The heirlooms that attract the most viewers are the Imperial Crown of Austria, the Crown of the Holy Roman Empire and Roger II's Mantle.

This sumptuous relic definitely fascinates modern man. It was created in that fabulous Sicilian era that saw rough northern warriors sweetened by eastern civilization and pursue—in their taste for beautiful things, in their tolerance and hard work—the myth of the Golden Age.

How was the mantle made? What intricate events brought it so far from Sicily? Roger II's mantle is exceptional because of the silk, the gold and pearls adorning it, for the wealth of the composition and its precise symbolism, for the inscription that transforms it into a document of the era in which it was made in the Royal Workshop (Tiraz) of Palermo, that is, in the great artisan laboratory that was inside the Royal Palace from the time of the Emirs. This laboratory, however, became well known and prestigious only in the era of and by the will of Roger II himself. Numerous embroiderers who had learned their art in Corinth and Thebes were brought to Palermo in 1147, after the expedition led by George of Antioch. In the Palermo workshop, the women showed their abilities, especially in the spinning of figurative motifs that they probably shared with the Sicilian embroiderers.

The luxury that surrounded the Norman court demanded an intense work rhythm for the Palermitan laboratory: from the workshop came out not only the ornaments needed by the King, the dignitaries and their guests, but also the cloth for the servants and horse saddles that always had in their design some gold threads. The gold, sewn in the cloth was the dazzling symbol of the dignity, power, and prestige of the Norman monarchy. And the hand-made objects of Palermo were well known and appreciated in all Europe for their characteristics. The historian Ugo Falcando was referring to one of the most luminous realizations of the Palermitan court when he wrote that he "could not ignore the laboratories where they spin and weave silk of various hues, from green to red, whose beautiful tone glows before your face, the damasks shaped as flowers, as shields, as round bubbles, the cloths in which the gold is woven with the silk and the multiform variety of the painting is made to come alive with inlaid gems." Filippo Pottino rightly noted in his remarks at the International Conference of Roger Studies, held in Palermo in 1954, that Ugo Falcando's note seemed to him: "The most felicitous and faithful description of Roger's mantle."

The mantle of Roger II was perhaps the masterpiece created by the Palermo workshop: on a vast expanse of purple silk—the color for regality—there is a rich decoration with gold threads executed by expert hands. The purple background makes the stylized figures that are the same on both sides stand out: a haughty lion, with its chest out and its long tail in the air and a camel, subdued by the lion and lying on the ground, is torn apart by the lion's claws as it exhales its last breath. The symbolism of the bestiary has a precise political significance: the Norman lion has subdued the Muslim camel. At the center of the composition, there is a tall palm tree with long geometrically extended leaves with symmetrical bunches of dates.

Lions and palm trees: the style is the same as the mosaics in Roger's Room in the Royal Palace of Palermo. In these mosaics, too, the lions have a tail standing in the air and the palm tree with a long trunk has leaves geometrically extended and bunches of dates hanging from it. Probably one of the creators of the mosaics furnished to the weavers of the workshop the cartoon for the royal mantle with the unmistakable intent of exalting Roger's victory and the defeat of Islam on Sicilian soil.

The artists of the laboratory worked strenuously to make the precious mantle perfect, one of a kind in the world. The extremely gifted embroiderers decorated the purple-colored silk made on the same looms of the workshop with non metallic golden threads (made with very thin leather strips immersed in liquid gold) which they pinned to the cloth itself with silken threads, using a technique known as "punta ad arazzo". They allowed the silken background to show the anatomical elements of the lion and camel and the other decorations and enriched the mantle with little pearls called "margaritae"; they finally placed two medallions with decorations in varnish on geometric motifs inside a frame of filigree and precious stones.

Along the external edge, they embroidered the following inscription

Roger II's coronation mantle in Vienna.

in gold, in Kufic letters: "Manufactured in the Royal Workshop where happiness and honor, well being and perfection, merit and excellence have their residence; may it be the place where one enjoys good reception, rich profits, great liberality, great splendor, good reputation, magnificence, as well as the fulfillment of vows and hopes; may the days and nights there pass with endless pleasure, without change in honor, with fidelity, diligent activity, happiness and long prosperity, submission and work that is appropriate. In the capital of Sicily, the year 528." The year 528 refers to the Hegira and corresponds to 1134 of the Christian era.

The creators of the mantle, therefore, still spoke in the language of the vanquished and expressed themselves in an Arabic manner (cf. the computation of the year according to the Arabic tradition), but they praised, through their masterpiece which has defied the wear and tear of centuries, their Norman conquerors.

Why is the mantle found in Vienna? It was brought to Vienna in the year 1800 and remained there until 1938 when, by order of Hitler, the precious heirloom was transferred to Nuremberg. Only after the end of the war did it return to the Austrian Capital where it is today.

In 1938, on the eve of the Napoleonic-style theft by the head of the Third Reich, the mantle had been taken out of its display case—under unusual circumstances—and gently laid out on a large white sheet on the floor of the "Shatzkammer" hall in Vienna. It was part of an attempt to check on the state of preservation not so much of the mantle, but of the light green-colored silk lining that was composed of a cloth containing very complex geometrical motifs (serpents, stylized palm groves, birds), whose significance has escaped even the experts who addressed the subject during a conference devoted to the purpose.

A Sicilian scholar present at that reconnoitering was fortunate enough to hold the fabulous mantle on her shoulders so that others could observe the natural folds in the cloth. The scholar was Maria Accascina, author of art books and a specialist on ancient cloth, and she related her singular adventure in a note tucked away at the end of a volume on the jewelry of Sicily, published in Palermo in 1974. Accascina related that the director of the Vienna Museum had been urged to conduct the check by the Italian Minister Preziosi who had expressed the desire to see the famous heirloom without the hindrance of the glass enclosure.

On that occasion, Professor Accascina was asked with a smile to put Roger's embroidered golden gloves, but she immediately refused the offer almost with a sense of repulsion, but wearing the very heavy royal mantle for a few minutes was for her an unforgettable experience.

To tell this episode, we postponed explaining how Roger's mantle was taken away. It was the German Emperor Henry VI, the son of Frederick I, Barbarossa, and the husband of Constance of Hauteville who took the mantle, together with other treasures out of the Royal Palace of Palermo. After the death of Tancredi in 1194, as a way of underscoring the end of the Norman era, Henry VI who had descended in Sicily with his imperial troops, did not hesitate to enter the rooms that had belonged to Tancredi to take away precious objects and treasures. The same personage whom history marked with the name of "cruel," had Tancredi's tomb opened to take possession of the crown, scepter, and other regal ornaments. It was Henry VI, father of the future "stupor mundi," Frederick II, who had the treasures of the Royal Palace of Palermo, including Roger's mantle, brought to the underground rooms of the Trifels castle belonging to his brother Philip of Swabia, amassing a treasure that enhanced his power. The historian Ernst Kantorowicz, in his monumental work on Frederick II, wrote that one year after the birth of Frederick and from Henry VI's taking possession of Sicily, there arrived to the imperial castle of Trifels in Germany (1195), "a caravan of one hundred fifty mules loaded with gold, silk, gems and precious objects, and it was made known that this was only a part of the booty taken by the Emperor from the Norman Palace of Palermo. Soon after that, Henry was advised by a messenger sent by Constance of Hauteville that "Roger's entire treasure had been found, thanks to an old servant who showed the secret door that led to it."

Afterwards, the regalia and all the other treasures were kept in Nuremberg and then, to avoid Napoleon's thievery, they were hidden in Rechensburg. Finally, in 1800, the heirlooms were displayed in the Imperial Treasure room n Vienna.

The circle concludes here. Roger's mantle never returned to Palermo at the end of the first world war, as requested by a Sicilian petition sent to the national commission for war reparations, because the theft after so many centuries was covered by time limitations. But that old and precious heirloom, jealously kept in the heart of the Hapsburg capital, still speaks, where the middle European culture has its deepest roots, a universal language that everyone can understand.

Charles V in Sicily

In the heart of old Palermo, in Bologni square, there stands the fortunate statue of a king who, perhaps uniquely in the history of revolutions, has been respected twice by the rebelling population. It is the statue of the Spanish monarch Charles V, modeled in the first half of the seventeenth century by Scipione Li Volsi. From a high pedestal, the Monarch extends his right arm as he swears over the Gospel to "respect the constitutions, the chapters, the free duties of the Realm and especially the privileges of the City of Palermo." Owing to the sacred character of this gesture, the statue remained intact in 1848 and 1860, while other monuments and symbols of power fell to the fury of the people.

The oath frozen in bronze was taken on the morning of September 13, 1535 in the Norman Cathedral of Palermo in a festive atmosphere in the presence of an emotional crowd of people. Charles V had returned victorious from Tunis where he had dealt a serious blow to Islam in its weakest spot, and even if in years to come the conquest of the African coast of the Mediterranean was the source of many disappointments (the Turks continued to sack the shores of Christian countries until the Battle of Lepanto on October 7, 1571), no one doubted the valor and the daring of the "Greatest Prince of the Christians," known as "the World's Monarch".

These epithets were used by one of his advisers, the Piedmontese Mercurio Gattinara, who interpreted general feelings for this

Charles V, portrayed in the act of swearing.

young and powerful leader who was proclaimed King of Spain at the age of sixteen and at nineteen he was elected Emperor of the Holy Roman Empire of Germany and who had finally had the privilege, when he was only thirty years old, of receiving the iron crown of Italy and the gold crown of the Empire from Pope Clement VII.

Charles V arrived in Sicily accompanied by the prestige that derived from his deeds and his fortune, and the Sicilians, as Virgilio Titone insightfully pointed out, considered themselves satisfied with Spain's protection, certain that without this protection their land would have fallen into the hands of the infidels.

The welcome that the Sicilian cities reserved for Charles V, especially in Palermo, also expressed their gratitude to the Emperor for defeating their enemies on the other shore of the Mediterranean, thus reducing the danger of their feared pirate incursions along their coast.

The minute account of activities of the days between the summer and fall of 1535 is no longer available, but we have reports from writers of a later era who consulted diaries, now mostly lost, of those who lived through those events. Gregorio Leti is one of these writers. A rebellious and anti-conformist spirit who wrote a history of the Emperor at the end of the seventeenth century, Leti provided very colorful details while also displaying some irreverence.

We learn from Leti that the Emperor, "after traveling with favorable winds," landed in Trapani where he disbanded the fleet that had taken part in the African expedition, making sure that "everyone left laden with infinites spoils and a good number of slaves of both sexes." Charles V did not forget to send his wife Isabella "fifty very beautiful Turkish slaves aged between six and twenty years, and fifty of the most handsome males of the same age so that she could choose the ones she wanted and give the rest to her ladies in waiting as gifts." These were the customs of that age.

He stayed four days in Trapani. He started toward Palermo with an ample escort and the most intimate confidants, among whom the Duke of Alba, Don Ferrante Gonzaga, the Duke of Medinaceli, the Pope's Nuncio and his secretaries. In the woods of Partinico, the Emperor's party met with Simone Ventimiglia, the Marquis of Geraci and President of the Kingdom and with the principal Barons, all dressed with great pomp, surrounded by pages and horse handlers, to pay homage to the guest who was setting foot on Sicily for the first time.

There was a pause in Monreale where Charles V was obliged to spend eight days, more than he had planned to because the city of Palermo had requested a week to make preparations for the solemn homage to Africa's conqueror.

The entrance to the capital occurred on the morning of September 13. We rely on Leti again to describe the procession which opened with Christians former slaves in Africa, who had been freed by the Emperor's troops. The women walked in lines of fours, according to their ages and before all of them there was a "matron," holding a finely made crucifix in her hand. The men followed also in lines of fours according to their ages. The freed slaves were guests of Palermo for a few days and then they were sent to their homes at the expense of the kingdom.

"The cavalcade was marvelous," commented the writer. Following the freed slaves, a platoon of one hundred citizens dressed like the infantry of the African expedition, but with this difference: instead of being made of cheap cloth, the uniforms were made of precious silk. The one hundred soldiers were all young men of the same height and almost the same age so as to produce a harmonious visual effect.

The official point of the meeting of Charles V with the capitol of the Kingdom occurred exactly below the gate that had provided entry into the city for a century and was then called New Gate (*Porta Nuova*). The Monarch was received by the clergy, the nobility and the Senate under a brocade baldaquin decorated with gold and with two-headed eagles. Four noblemen approached Charles V and presented him with a splendid white horse whose saddle was estimated to have cost one hundred thousand *scudi*. Charles dismounted his horse and mounted the other one with the help of those present who held the horse's bridles and staff. The Emperor donated his horse, inviting the people near him to choose a new owner for it. The artillery and the festively pealing bells were heard at the same time. The onlooking crowd burst into a long applause.

As a remembrance of this moment, the Palermitan Senate decided to rebuild the gate decorating it with friezes and symbols, among which the four colossal defeated "Turks," two of whom are shown with arms cut off, recalling the exalting African victory.

As the clergy at the entrance sang festive hymns, the Emperor with an honor escort reached the nearby Norman Cathedral. Dismounting, Charles V entered the church welcomed by the Bishop of Mazara. He concentrated in prayer for a moment in the silent church and then approaching the Bishop who handed him the Gospels, swore solemnly before the multitudes that he would preserve the privileges of the City and of the Kingdom.

After the ceremony was finished, Charles V mounted his horse and, followed by his honor escort, under a baldaquin of gold brocade, crossed the Marble Way decorated with friezes and arches that exalted the leader's military victory. He reached thus AiutamiCristo Palace, near Porta Termini, where he stayed. After three consecutive days, inside a fenced-in space especially erected in the Fieravecchia square, the most able jousters of the Kingdom, among whom the famous Pietro Ribera who won the competition, vied against each other in daring feats in homage to the guest of honor in a climate of cheer and festivity.

After three days, Charles V asked for the festivities to end. He had called for a meeting of the Parliament for September 16 in the hall of the Steri Palace. It was one of the motives, if not the main one, for his coming to Palermo. The historian William Robertson, in his weighty history of the reign of Charles V, completely skipped the Sicilian sojourn of the Spanish monarch, even though that stop was not without consequence. The Emperor received from the three branches of the Sicilian Parliament, the Clergy, the Military and the Government Branches, not to mention the marquis, counts, barons and landowners, an exceptionally high donation of two hundred fifty thousand ducats as a contribution of the Kingdom for his military efforts in Africa and future campaigns in Europe.

The Parliament was conducted according to a particularly solemn ceremony. The Emperor on his throne, reached after climbing seven wide steps covered with red velvet, had at his feet the two Presidents of the Magna Curia and the Royal Patrimony. Lower down sat the Judges, the Fiscal Prosecutors, the Rational Masters and all the other functionaries of the Kingdom. Before him stood the representatives of the three Branches of Parliament and the ambassadors.

After the Emperor gave the nod, the Protonotary read the speech. The Monarch, he said, had always desired to come to Sicily, "a land of ancient bravery, of long-lasting fidelity," but he had been unable to do so. He asked for the Parliament's contribution "in view of the fact that the imperial treasury was nearly exhausted because of the efforts endured to protect the island and Christian faith. His Imperial Majesty was certain that the Parliament would make a generous and extraordinary contribution."

The meeting was adjourned right away. In the following days, the session continued in the residence of the host in the AiutamiCristo Palace. On September 22, the three branches had agreed to deposit into the imperial treasury 250 thousand ducats as an "extraordinary service." The sum was divided thus: 40 thousand from the Ecclesiastical Branch, 80 thousand from the Government Branch, 80 thousand from the Military Branch and 50 thousand from the titled noblemen. The entire sum would be payable within four months.

When Charles V accepted the donation, the Parliament asked him in exchange "to reform justice and other necessary things in this most faithful kingdom of his." Among the requests, that the Viceroys not remain in power more than four years so as not to become partial and develop adherences; reduction of the taxes on wheat; abolishment of the sale of appointments; restitution of the income assigned to it by King Alphonse to the University of Catania, for "if that income were lacking that main hearth of science on the island would be at risk of becoming extinct." They also asked the Emperor to establish "Thirty knighthoods in the chivalric Order of Saint James."

Charles V remained in Palermo for thirty days between "enjoyments and pomp," wrote Isidoro La Lumia. Gregorio Leti, the irreverent writer we quoted earlier, added that the thirty-five year old Emperor "particularly enjoyed the dances to the extent that he would pay some brief visits *incognito* to the most beautiful and important ladies very late at night, around two o'clock (during the day he was busy with his business). If he was chaste, he was much more modest and secretive."

Having put to rest the African campaign, and

Porta Nuova showing four Saracens symbolizing Charles V's victory over Islam.

filled up the imperial treasury, Charles V must have regarded his Palermitan sojourn as a very pleasant and relaxing parenthesis. "That was the moment," as Robertson wrote, "when he reached the apex of his glory. It was the most luminous era of his reign…His fame outshone that of all the other European monarchs."

In reality, Charles V found himself in very difficult situations that were beyond his means and he was able to face them with great effort relying with caution and cunning on his exceptional diplomatic abilities. When he died at age 58 in a monastery in Estremadura, with the signs of madness inherited from his mother *Juan la loca*, the slow decline of Spain began.

Palermo never forgot Charles' visit and, in fact, the likeness of the Monarch still stands not only in piazza Bologni, as we said, but also in one of the fifteenth century corners and in Carraffello square, on the façade of the Mazzarino Palace.

The Emperor himself did not forget his journey to Sicily, even though it was dictated by obvious motives. In 1548, in a letter addressed to Don Diego of Cordoba, as mentioned by La Placa in a book published in 1736, warned him to have particular regard for the privileges of Palermo. "Our intention and will—Charles V wrote textually on that occasion—was and is to generally safeguard the privileges, the chapters, the rites and the good costumes of the whole realm, and in particular way those of the City of Palermo for the many, good services rendered to us."

Cagliostro, Palermitan and Cosmopolitan

The Palermitan adventurer named Cagliostro who coursed through the second half of the eighteenth century with high sounding names, was in reality a "pen draftsman"—that's the way he described himself at the beginning of his extraordinary career—and his real name was Giuseppe Balsamo.

He admitted that his name was Giuseppe Balsamo for the first time in a letter written after he was imprisoned in a cell in Castel Sant'Angelo. He was 46 years old then and he had been arrested in Rome on December 27, 1789. But his confession was not known right away. In fact, during his peregrinations, which had taken him to European countries and areas of the Mediterranean, he had given numerous other names that he changed according to his whim: Marquis Pellegrini, Marquis D'anna, Count Balsamo, Count Fenix. However, the name with which the Palermitan is known and which has crossed centuries, becoming an adjective, is Count Alessandro Cagliostro. He took that name after the Masonic initiation that took place on April 2, 1777, in the Lodge *L'Esperante* of London which reported to the Grand Lodge of England.

The mystery of his identity lasted a long time and Balsamo-Cagliostro did all he could to keep it a secret. At this point, it behooves us to review the life of this most controversial traveler of the XVIII century who was one of the most notorious men of his time. Given the incredible sequence of the adventures, travels and encounters in which he was involved, this is not an easy task.

The son of a modest businessman, Giuseppe Balsamo was born on June 2, 1743 in the Albergheria section and precisely in a narrow street called Count Cagliostro Alley since 1869. He was baptized six days afterward in the Palermo Cathedral, as can be seen in the Registers of the parish chapel held in Incoronazione street.

In Balsamo's time the narrow passage between the two rows of houses was known as *via del Perciato* (Pierced street) after the name of a nearby tavern; later it came to be known as *via del Pisciato* (Pissed street), owing to a corruption of the word that ironically underscored the fact that the street had become an open cesspool. Giuseppe Balsamo fled this place—among the most secretive in Palermo—at a very young age.

Forced to leave his native city in a hurry following a swindle perpetrated against a jeweler named Marano, Cagliostro reached Rome after some perilous stops.

A short time afterward, he married a young woman named Feliciana, daughter of a bell maker, and began to travel with her throughout Europe, committing feats that used the entire continent as a stage.

He had a natural talent for swindling. He was cunning and intelligent, which made up for his limited education. He had a gift for words and was able to attract members of a society of powdered wigs, sensitive to superstition and magic. He knew how to influence people willing to listen to him. With such gifts openly displayed, he triumphed during the best years of his human adventure in an age that was not yet open to the Enlightenment. He had numerous involvements: he hoodwinked old ladies looking for the youth elixir; in Strasbourg he preyed on a wealthy and naïve man of the cloth as was the Cardinal of Rohan; with his wily arts, he seduced the Polish Prince Ponicki who was, as Cagliostro himself, a lover of alchemy and evoker of demons.

Giuseppe Balsamo, alias Count Cagliostro.

Giuseppe Balsamo had learned the rudiments of alchemy as a novice in the monastery of the Fatebenefratelli monks of Caltagirone where he was brought when he was twelve years old. At the request of his mother, who had become a widow, and who wanted to see her son out of the streets, the Head of the order took him to the monastery. Alchemy, together with the science of herbs, became in his later years the tool that made it possible for the enterprising young man to improvise cures and play with divinations and the occult. His stay in Russia was based on his exploitation of the occult, but he was unsuccessful in his attempt to charm Catherine the Great who in fact made fun of him in her writing.

Cagliostro, however, was extraordinarily successful in Strasbourg where he was hailed as a healer and a benefactor, affecting cures that the medical profession found irritating. His lucky star followed him to Paris where enthusiastic crowds welcomed him and people made engravings of his likeness and painted it even on fans. Nevertheless, his decline began in Paris. He was implicated, perhaps innocently, in the famous "Necklace Affair" and was imprisoned in the Bastille together with his wife. They were both released nine months afterward when they were found not guilty. Shortly after that, in London, where he went after his expulsion from France, he stunned everyone by prophesying that the Bastille would become a public promenade. After that, his descent into hell became unstoppable. To please his wife who wanted to see her parents, he traveled to Rome, then the capital of the Vatican State, which was hostile to outside influences and ever vigilant against anticlerical, revolutionary, and Masonic infiltrations. He unwisely organized a Masonic séance to introduce the so-called "Egyptian Rite" that he had founded. This thoughtlessness was fatal for him and even his wife accused him "to clear her conscience". He was arrested, tried, and condemned to death as a heretic, heresiarch, and a follower of magic and promoter of masonry.

His sentence to death was commuted to life imprisonment by Pious VI and he was sent to the inaccessible fortress of Saint Leo. There, the untamed prisoner spent four years and four months of suffering, and there, he finally died on August 26, 1795. Today, our modern conscience still finds the manner of the adventurer's death repugnant. He was an adventurer, but the Marquis of Villabianca from Palermo on a page of his diary of 1791, did not hesitate in defining him "a sublime intelligence".

How did Cagliostro manage to keep his true identity a jealously guarded secret for so long?

Cagliostro tried to throw people off track when he introduced himself during his detention at the Bastille as an unlucky pilgrim in the streets of the world. He gave his defense lawyer, the attorney Thilorier, a biographical sketch published by an anonymous printer that contained the following premise that speaks volumes about the notoriety of the prisoner: "The memoirs of Count Cagliostro attracted a multitude of readers, naturally. As soon as they were published, they became the subject of every conversation…"

The document is revealing. Having stated that he was "known in all of Europe and in a large part of Africa and Asia," he wrote: " I do not know where I was born and the parents who brought me into this world. I spent the years of my childhood in Medina, in Arabia; I was raised there with the name of Acharat. I lived in the palace of the Mufti Salahayim." He also mentioned that he thought he had been orphaned when he was three months old and that he may have been born in Malta. Needless to say, these are all lies. This document is interesting because it was written when Cagliostro was at the apex of his success and the beginning of his decline. The identification of the fake count with the Palermitan Giuseppe Balsamo was made public by Antonio Bivona, a Palermitan baron and attorney for France in Sicily, at the same time as the publication of Balsamo's memoirs in Paris. He had managed to compile a genealogical tree of Giuseppe Balsamo, relying on the fact that the Cagliostros from Messina were related to the Palermitan Balsamos and that a certain Vincenza Cagliostro (written Cachiostro due to an error in transcription) had been a godmother at the baptism of the infant Balsamo.

The genealogical tree was promptly dispatched to Paris. It was shown to Wolfgang Goethe when the great poet went to Sicily. He wanted to have confirmation that what was already suspected was actually true and that Count Alessandro Cagliostro was none other than Giuseppe Balsamo. Nevertheless, the German traveler was moved when he visited the adventurer's mother and sister on seeing the dignified poverty of the two women and when he returned to Germany, he sent them a sum of money that Balsamo's relatives believed had been sent by the adventurer.

The life of the Palermitan in the Fortress of Saint Leo is mysterious and full of surprises. The event surrounding his death and his burial in de-consecrated ground, as willed by the papal authorities, is also mysterious. In the death certificate it was specifically written that he had been buried on the extreme point of the mountain that looks toward the west, almost at an equal distance from the fortresses commonly known as the "Palazzetto" and the "Casino," normally used to house the guards. But an attempt to identify the place of burial conducted in the nineteen sixties was unsuccessful. Later, scholar Nevio Martini conducted another search in collaboration with the Saint Leo authorities and wrote a detailed account of it in the *Domenica del Corriere* on December 8, 1963. But this attempt also did not produce credible results because the excavation revealed some animal bones together with some human remains that were difficult to date.

Even today in the year 2000, the mystery of the unknown tomb of Cagliostro remains and it arouses curiosity about the unique human events regarding an uncomfortable character from the second half of the eighteenth century. At any rate, what is the sense in looking for Cagliostro's remains? For a long time people believed that seeing the documents held in the Vatican archives about the trial held against the magician by the Inquisition would have been enlightening. Recently, however, we took note of the reply given by the Vatican archivist to someone who was enquiring about the documents. The reply stated that the dossier contained only the *Compendium* by Giovanni Barberi and suggested that the papers regarding Cagliostro could be in Paris following the sack of the Vatican archives perpetrated by order of Napoleon.

Thus, after the burning of the letters, papers, and documents in Minerva square, taken from Cagliostro at the time of his arrest in Rome, there seems to be nothing left to uncover.

A Magician in Cefalù

In the early morning of April 14, 1920, a tepid day in Spring, the people of Cefalù saw a strange group of foreigners walk on the main thoroughfare of the city in the company of a well known local person. A man with a shaved head was part of the group. He was just forty five years old, but he looked older on account of his massive body. He was dressed in an eccentric way and that aroused attention in a city of ten thousand people that was usually visited by tourists who wanted to see the famous Norman cathedral.

There were two young women accompanying the stranger, both wearing flimsy dresses that allowed the youth of their bodies to be visible. One of them held a little girl by the hand who could not have been older than four. The group showed no curiosity for their surroundings, did not look around and, as they followed their guide, did not make eye contact with the people looking at them. The four of them walked at a brisk pace through the inhabited part of town and when they reached the last houses, at the point where the road to Messina began, they turned right and continued on an upward path amidst olive trees and prickly pears until they reached a flat expanse in a section called Santa Barbara, where there was a small, isolated one-floor house that was their destination. Who was that stranger who had come to Cefalù with his women? People learned after a while that the man with the shaved head was Aleister Crowley who had come down from Naples. He had identified Cefalù through the Chi-

Aleister Crowley with one of his concubines and her child.

nese oracle, the *Yi King,* eliminating other localities of the South, so that the mild climate through many months of the year would help to cure him of his bronchitis and asthma, two diseases that had afflicted him for a long time in his native England.

Aleister Crowley has been considered a magician, an anti-Christ, a devil, an immoral witch doctor, the most perverse man on earth, a Satan lover, a guru of the occult, a creator and follower of appalling rites. He certainly was an individual who possessed a perverse talent and an unsettling personality. He was born at the height of Queen Victoria's reign on October 12, 1875, in Warwickshire County. He was a cynical and rebellious character from an early age. He had an obsession with sex and he rejected the morality of his time.

Crowley wearing one of his eccentric costumes.

After he found a house to rent in place of the little hotel where he had stayed initially, he planned to accomplish his "Great Work" in the temple he built in Cefalù, calling it "The Abbey of Thelema." Thelema was for him a key word that identified the monastery "made for the honest delight of the body and the spirit" in which Gargantua, the character created by Rabelais in his work, could live according to the rule: "Do as you please." He adopted the same rule and as soon as he took possession of the house in Cefalù, the first thing he did was to trace a circle that he considered magic in the first room and drew a pentagram over it.

With the natural talent of a painter, he drew images of he-goats and naked women on the walls, representing in a vivid way the nature of the magic and orgiastic rites that he expected to celebrate with the assistance of the two women who shared his house. He signed these colored drawings Aleister Crowley with the A of his name larger than the other letters and with the rounded legs of the letter simulating a phallic emblem. In the center of the room, he put a table that he pretentiously called: "The Threshold of the Great Beast."

One of the two women who had come with him to Cefalù was called "The Concubine of the Beast" and the other "The Scarlet Woman," perhaps because of the reddish color of her hair. The little girl whose name was Anna died in a Palermo hospital soon after their arrival. She was the daughter of one of the women.

Crowley quickly began his magic-orgiastic rites of which he was a master. They were derived primarily from his belonging to the *Ordo Templi Orientis* (OTO for the members) that had been founded in 1896 by a wealthy industrialist Karl Kellner, who placed yoga and sexual magic at the center of their esoteric activities.

Using a flamboyant choreography, Crowley organized processions wearing weird vestments around his residence. The two women who had come with him were joined by others after some time. In the summer months they walked to the beach and they bathed without clothes, shocking the population that watched them from afar. Even when he came down alone, wearing flamboyant costumes and walking with a long cane, Crowley scandalized and evoked fear, especially in women, who often crossed themselves when they chanced to cross his path.

The people of Cefalù were attracted and repulsed at once by the mysterious character. Thus many learned about the obscene rites that were conducted in the Abbey of Thelema and of the repeated use of drugs imported directly from England. Crowley left his house in Cefalù only a few times. Once, he boarded a train in Palermo directed to Paris where he went presumably to settle his economic difficulties which, having squandered a fortune, had become serious. Another time he boarded a ship directed to Tunis. But after a few days or weeks, he always returned to his house in Cefalù where he lived with the two women who came with him and with other guests who would arrive from time to time.

After staying in England, the British press harshly attacked Crowley, accusing him of "exploiting unhappy people," of conducting "perverse rituals," and denouncing "the delirium of an insane criminal, driven mad by his depravity." In reality, Crowley behaved exactly as he had defined himself, a "Great Beast." He began his rites by slaughtering a dog or a cat, forcing those who participated to drink the blood of the sacrificed animals. He imposed extravagant rules on the guests of the Abbey of Thelema which consisted of self punishment. For every infraction, the guilty party was to carve his own arm using a big knife that was always handy.

A complaint to the British Consul General in Palermo did not have any effect on his behavior nor did the attacks by British newspapers until April 23, 1923—at the beginning of the Fascist era—when a police agent came to his house and asked him to follow him to the police station. There he was handed the order of expulsion from Italy, signed by the Minister of the Interior, as someone who had disturbed the public order.

He left alone, abandoning his women in Cefalù without any means of support. He boarded a ship headed for Tunis, but he did not stay in Africa for long. Shortly thereafter he sailed to Marseilles from where he continued his restless wandering. In 1939, he was expelled from France as well and forced to go back to England. He then went to Portugal where he simulated a suicide after he tried to sell, like a novel Cagliostro, pills that he called "Long-Life Elixir". He had time to write and publish esoteric treatises among which his masterpiece entitled *Magick*, a book that combined alchemy with sexual magic and oriental mystery cults. He returned to England one more time, where he died on December 1, 1947, exhausted and poisoned. He died of degeneration of his myocardial muscle, and acute bronchitis, as was noted on his death certificate.

In the testament written in 1931, he had asked that his ashes be sealed in the megalithic rock of Cefalù, a place bound to Mediterranean mythology and to rites of the occult. But after his body was cremated his remains were buried in the English city of Brighton, after a recitation of an "agnostic requiem" he had composed.

As a priest of the occult and a master of perversion, Crowley was probably insane in the clinical sense of the word, a prisoner in the course of his tormented existence of the character with which he had chosen to identify: the Anti-Christ on earth. His perverse fame induced the writer Somerset Maugham to use Crowley as the model for his novel *The Magician*. In 1955, the American expert on human sexuality Alfred Charles Kinsey tried to understand the secrets of Crowley's mysterious personality by coming to Cefalù. But when he entered the house on the hill, he saw only what was left of Crowley's erotic drawings, half covered over by thick, white paint.

The ethnologist Fosco Maraini who accompanied the scientist, together with a few friends, related that the night before he had seen the remains of a black cat with a crushed skull in front of the door. This was interpreted by the frightened little group as clear evidence of black magic.

Cefalù has not forgotten the mysterious character. The town has acquired the house on the hill to make it into a museum. Through the years a local collector, Pietro Sajia, has been able to assemble a thick documentation on the Englishman's stay there, including furniture and fixtures used in the Abbey of Thelema. These are the premises for the establishment of a museum to remember Crowley's stay in Cefalù. He was a *provocateur* that the esoteric world has not forgotten.

In February 1997, the Cefalù Tourist Board organized a convention that was attended by specialists in the esoteric arts such as the American J. Gordon Melton, the Swiss Peter Koenig and the Italian Massimo Introvigne, all of whom were interested in digging into the mystery of a Satanist who is still considered today a renovator of magic thinking. Crowley's influence on today's contemporary magic environment is considerable and at least one hundred members of the "New magic movements" have direct connections with him.

The guru of the occult, who lived between the nineteenth and twentieth centuries has followers inspired by his perverse teaching. The internet devotes a large space to his figure. There is even a video available. The images show Crowley and the paintings that remain in the house in Cefalù where he lived.

The Abbey of Thelema is a memento of the passage through Sicily of the man who embodied the devil on earth. That is why on this Mediterranean island people still recall in awe this dark minister of perverse rituals.

The Irony of the Catanesi

Entering the imposing gates of Bellini Gardens through Via Etnea, I climbed the gentle ramp that led to the boulevards and to the round pool in whose center a vertiginous spout that pours down white foam on the water as it falls. The weather on this Sunday morning is radiant, the straight avenue traced in 1693 by don Giuseppe Lanza, Duke of Camastra, the Viceroy's military architect, is full of people walking and arguing, but does not seem to go beyond Garibaldi's statue portrayed with his poncho by the Roman Ettore Ferrari. The statue that was refused by the Uruguayan Government because they had wanted the Leader of the Thousand riding on a horse, has stood at the point of bifurcation with via Caronda since 1914.

Moms and dads together with their little ones swarm into the Park with its large clock set in the green. Two tall palm trees stand vigilant on the iron rim of the Palace high on the hill. The children and their parents approach the vendors' benches to buy colored balloons and sweets.

I look carefully at the pool and I can't see the swans that moved

Catania with Mt. Etna looming above it. In the foreground, Bellini Gardens.

with elegance and dignified slowness, as I remembered well. I wanted to understand why they were not there and I had an inkling. I turned to the man sitting at the nearest table and asked him "Are the swans not here perhaps because of the Aviary?" His answer was precise and immediate: "What aviary? Are you kidding? They stole them. And they even took the monkeys!"

It was true, but there was in his cutting remark a sense of derision, an expression of spontaneous mocking. It was as though in his sharp retort there emerged the Catania of old which through the open-voweled and clear voice of its inhabitants knows how to reflect on the facts of life, the minutest daily events and turn everything into mockery and sarcasm. It is the irony that's contained in the DNA of old-time *Catanesi*; it is also the irony that Brancati used when he made unrelenting fun of the sentimental life of his *Bell'Antonio*. It is the Catania of Ercole Patti who related from precise memories how "The lava stone paved Via Etnea on which girls, men of letters, and ironic and quibbling lawyers grew old." It is the Catania where the exhilarating characters created by Giuseppe Villaroel lived. But the city that welcomes the Sunday crowds is also the eighteenth century Catania intelligently illustrated by the architect Francesco Fichera. It is the Catania that is embodied by Via Etnea as it passes through the Four Corners and reaches Bellini Gardens.

Beyond the palaces of the nobility, the sumptuous Baroque churches, the imposing public buildings, you can see the "imperfect megalopolis" that was described by the historian Giuseppe Giarrizzo, with an image that gives us the idea of the vastness of the city that lies at the foot of the largest volcano in Europe: a chaotic and exciting metropolis made up of orbital roads, residential neighborhoods, nationally important industrial parks and little villages that make up the territory of the "Milan of the South."

Walking along Via Etnea, the eighteenth century city reveals its urban fabric stubbornly rebuilt after the disastrous cataclysm that occurred at the end of the seventeenth century that caused the death of sixteen thousand people out of its twenty five thousand inhabitants.

As always, the liveliness of the people of Catania finds expression in the leisure walk along the elegant living room of the city on Via Etnea. And with a little attention to historical memory you can see again the glories of the past in the chosen places. At the Four Corners, there was once the Circolo Unione where Giovanni Verga, as an old gentleman tired of his Milanese success, went every afternoon. Saverio Fiduccia, a discreet writer of Catanese events, remembered him "buried in a red velvet lounge chair, with his cane upon his knees, his tube hat on his head and a cigarette in his mouth: a handsome man, in spite his eighty years of age, with white drooping moustaches and stern look."

Further down, in University Square you can see Sangiuliano Palace with its multicolored façade built by Giovan Battista Vaccarini, in whose courtyard there are four slabs of marble in memory of the illustrious guests of the past who stayed there: Carlo Umberto Oddone, Archduke of Savoy in 1862; The Archduke Ludovico and the Archduchess Maria Teresa of Austria in 1880; Umberto I and his Queen Margherita in 1881, Edward VII of England with Queen Alexandra and the Empress of Russia, Maria Fedorovna in 1909.

A view of the Church of Saint Agatha and the famous elephant, symbol of Catania.

There are fixed point of reference in Catania's reality. These are the places that give the city its precise identity: the smoking cone of Mt. Etna, which is almost a symbol of the volcanic character of the *Catanesi*; Bellini's house and Giovanni Verga's that have remained almost exactly the same since the time the composer and the writer lived in them; the feast for the Patron Saint, Agatha, which still today moves the crowds; the monument to Vincenzo Bellini which sums up the cult shared by the people for the musical genius, a cult that is sublimated in the gastronomic recipe of "Pasta alla Norma"; finally there is the so-called "Villa," Bellini Gardens, comprising seventy thousand square meters of park land, born out of a whim to build an eighteenth century labyrinth by Prince Ignazio Paternò Castello of Biscari. It became and still is the lungs of this sleepless city of the legendary Elephant.

And yet modernity has breathed for a long time in the body of this thrice-reborn city. Old historic hotels are no longer here or have been transformed. The hotel on Via Etnea, that reproduced the coin of the ancient Greek city on the door to each room now belongs to a hotel chain. The Rosticceria Giardini on Via Etnea which was famous for its *arancine* closed its doors in 1958. The Swiss pastry shop of Alessandro Caviezel that was open from 1914 to 1976 is no longer there. But those who know how to read the history of the city, not the history of the ancient Roman amphitheater or the spa beneath the Cathedral, but the history of the nineteenth century that is closer to us, can still see the shadow of the temperamental poet of *Giobbe*, Mario Rapisardi, who walked down to the center of town with his black hat pressed upon his head, greeted by his students and mocked by the *Catanesi* because his beautiful wife Giselda Fojanesi, a northerner, had slipped under the sheets with Giovanni Verga.

He was an illustrious cuckold in the Catania that does not forgive human frailties, the Catania of the mime Angelo Musco who with his grating laughter and easily understood gestures transformed tragedy into jokes.

The Allure of Etna

The Sicilian dictionary pays tribute to Etna, the largest active volcano in Europe, noting that "A Muntagna," especially in the eastern part of Sicily, identifies the smoking cone, frequently covered with snow, that dominates the city of Catania with its imposing size (3,350 meters high). Its height is variable, however, because of the sinking and collapsing of internal walls of the central crater that sinks towards unknown abysses. These are connected to a hot point of the earth, in which considerable quantities of lava are pushed from the deepest layers of the globe towards the earth's mantle. A unique specimen, therefore, that has always inspired those who have seen it from afar or have struggled to reach the mouth of the rocky monster that covers an area of 1600 square kilometers and has a circumference of about 150 kilometers.

Most people are amazed, astonished, and, at times helpless before this marvel of nature. People often quote the Greek poet Pindar, who concisely defined Etna as "The column of the sky". However, many other ancient authors have described the mountain's peculiarity, with words that confirm the uniqueness of the event, of being quiet and then suddenly spewing fire and lava.

In 475 AD, the Athenian tragic poet Aeschylus watched from the steps of the vast Greek theater of Siracusa the first performance of his work *Le Etnee*, written by request from the tyrant of the city Gelon I, who wanted to celebrate in this way a nearby military outpost of his. The text of the play was lost, but the topic confirms the fascination with all that revolved around the volcano, named Etna by the Greeks, which means "Burning Mountain."

In the Roman period, Virgil described in the *Aeneid* the adventurous passage of Aeneas on a boat that sailed close to the coastline of eastern Sicily. The sailors saw Etna "that at times spews a black cloud in the sky," and at the same time they heard from afar "the deep groan of the sea". In 1184, sailing through the Strait of Messina, the Andalusian-Arab traveler Ibn Giubair saw from afar "the mountain of fire, that is, the famous volcano of Sicily" before his boat was shipwrecked. In the 17th century, the Englishman George Sandys wrote in his reportage about the "Queen of the Mediterranean" and its big volcano.

When Sicily, in the 18th century, entered the circuit of the great travelers, after the inclusion of the island in the Italian Grand Tour, Etna was reached almost always with difficulty, but those who made it to the summit described the enchantment of seeing the volcano up close. At the end of the 18th century, climbing all the way to the mouth of the crater, the German Baron Riedesel enjoyed "the most broad and most beautiful view that you can possibly imagine" from up there. In the same period, Lazzaro Spallanzani, a scientist, was enthused before the "burning volcano". In the 19th century, two more men of science, the abbot Francesco Ferrara and Carlo Gemmellaro, expressed in their accounts their surprise before that impressive natural scenario. The former considered the summit of Etna to be "the most superb observatory offered to man" and Carlo Gemmellaro felt excited in observing the spectacle offered by the "most ancient volcano mentioned by history." Still in the 19th century, the Frenchman Guy de Maupassant described "the prodigious, frightening abyss, the monstrous chasm of the crater."

Towards the end of the 20th century, the writer and philologist Maria Corti, who departing from her hometown of Milan visited the crater many times in the summer, described the mountain that towers over Catania as "the most mythical of all volcanoes". She was referring to the legends that over the course of centuries were fueled by visions of fairies, wizards, and heroes, gigantic monsters and underground caves; the most fervent repertoire of the imagination. You cannot forget that Etna was considered the forge of the god Vulcan, as well as the home of the giant Cyclops with only one eye; monsters of mythology, one of which, Polyphemus, was deceived by the cunning Ulysses, as we learned from reading one of the better known episodes of a classic of the Greek world.

Fulco Pratesi recently made a sharp observation: "Except for Mount Fuji in Japan, there is no other volcano in the world that has influenced the landscape, the history, and the life of surrounding populations more than Etna." It's true. The greatest European landscape artists of the 17th and 18th centuries painted the inhabited part of Catania putting Mount Etna, spewing fire and flames in the background, perhaps not respecting the proportions of the mountain and giving it a fanciful profile, at times very different from the real one. However, it is a justified deformation rising from the desire to give a physical face to a sublime locality.

From a geological point of view, Etna rests along the fault lines of the European and African plates. Therefore, the volcanism of Etna that generates lava flows is part of this mysterious morphological context.

Its base rises from the Ionic coast and holds up an immense cone: the highest mountain peak in Italy, if you exclude the Alps. It is one of the most active volcanoes in the world, with at least 150 recorded eruptions. The oldest one occurred probably in 693 BC, but the most disastrous in history was that of 1693 AD, which lasted four months, during which from the enormous crack opened in the area of Nicolosi nearly a million cubic meters of lava was spewed. Twenty-seven thousand homes were leveled by a river of magma that reached the sea. The awesome flow, after destroying in its passage fields and villages, reached Catania, altering the seventeenth century look of the city.

There have been numerous eruptions in times closer to us; they have at times cut off roads and swallowed houses, but they have not caused any fatalities. For this, it has been said that Etna is a good volcano, also because the lava very often pours out into the immense Valle del Bove, a providential receptacle that seems to have been created on purpose by nature to receive the incandescent magma.

The Valley of the Ox deserves a longer treatment. It is one of the many marvels that Etna offers. The enormous amphitheater has a perimeter of 18 kilometers and occupies an area of 37 square kilometers. The depression, covered with lava from different recorded eruptions, constitutes one of the wildest natural environments on our planet.

A view of Mt. Etna in contrast with the blooming bouganivillea.

One of the most frequent phenomena of the volcano is the ejection of lapilli. When they are emitted by the central crater, forming umbrella-like fountains of fire visible from great distances, they represent a tourist attraction that can be seen from far away. Taormina constitutes a privileged balcony for the extraordinary sight. But those who manage to climb up the mountain through organized excursions are able to enjoy different landscapes, always of varied nature and always breathtaking.

At the base of the volcano there is the forest that now is part of the "Parco dell'Etna," a nature reserve of nearly 60,000 hectares, created in 1982 and protected by a very rigid legislation. This uncontaminated green world includes authentic vegetable monuments, such as long-living gigantic trees. The best known is "The Chestnut Tree of a Hundred Horses," so named because during a storm, the immense branches provided shelter to a queen and the numerous carriages in her retinue. The park is the uncontaminated kingdom and refuge of the golden eagle, the peregrine falcon, the wildcat, and the long-eared owl. It is also a territory where shrubs grow that can't be found anywhere else. The silence of wide-open spaces is at times broken by the whistle of an old-time little train. It's the Circumetnea, a slow-moving train that links the towns nearest to the summit and makes a very attractive excursion possible.

Further up, where mechanical vehicles can't reach, there is a thicket of birch trees and climbing even more you see dense broom shrubs. Above that a vast kingdom of silence, covered with volcanic ash and battered by imperious winds, opens up. It is a majestic but desolate landscape, that foreshadows the loneliness and magnificence of the solitary summit.

It is the same enchantment that in every time period has seduced those who have approached the giant that the Arabs called "Mongibello," from the word *gebel*, which means precisely "mountain:" the absolute mountain, the mountain, *par excellence*.

The last notions on Etna deal with its geology. The Sicilian volcano, moving slowly at the speed of a few centimeters per year, is slipping toward the Ionic Sea. It's the result of an immense underground landslide verified by means of very sophisticated, new-generation instruments. But obviously, today nobody can notice these minute movements that are constantly monitored by seismographs capable of registering even the weakest telluric phenomena, and by the geodetic network that detects variations in the inclination of the mountain's slopes. These instruments make it possible to establish the slope from which the magma may flow.

Scholars of the International Institute of Volcanology watch over Etna by flying around the perimeter of the mountain with a helicopter. In short, the Sicilian volcano is kept under special surveillance. The scientific interest shown by the great volcanologists who have studied it, by taking long and strenuous walks over a rough terrain fraught with perils, is evidence of this. Haroun Tazieff, the scholar of Polish origin who passed away in 1988, used to lower himself inside the crater, when it was inactive, challenging the whims of an unpredictable creature, to study more closely the phenomena taking place in the depths. The Swiss Alfred Rittmann, another illustrious volcanologist of the 20th century who directed the Institute of Volcanology, was one of the first, when Etna was still observed with rudimentary instruments, to support the need for a network of permanent and automatic observations. He, among other things, studied the Valley of the Ox, formulating the hypothesis that the colossal valley was the result of the collapse of summit portions of the volcano that occurred in remote times.

Science monitors Etna, and this surveillance constitutes a guarantee because a timely alert can make known in advance the possibility of a reawakening of its eruptive activity, perhaps as disastrous as the one that devastated a large portion of Sicily in 1693.

In the meantime, the big mountain, visible from many mountain localities of the island, still continues to fascinate those who have the chance to get to know it, especially those who have the necessary energy to follow the treacherous roads that lead to the summit, more than three thousand meters high.

The Eco of Bellini's Melodies

Inside a modest mezzanine apartment of a princely palace in Catania (the Eighteenth century residence of the Gravinas), the intense presence of a man said to be the greatest European musical genius of the nineteenth century, Vincenzo Bellini, can still be felt among the furniture and objects that belonged to him, even though he only lived there during his childhood and early adolescence. In fact, he was not even eighteen when his grandfather, a musician who was also named Vincenzo, introduced him to the Dukes of San Martino in their drawing rooms, who obtained from the city's administration some financial support so he could continue his studies in the San Sebastiano Institute in Naples. It was only in 1832, in a brief interval between two artistic engagements, that Bellini returned to his native home, which has been transformed into a museum that still preserves the look of a private residence. You almost get the sensation of violating privacy, after crossing the paved courtyard, and climbing the stone steps that take you to the three rooms and the three small spaces, where the Bellini family lived. This impression remains when visiting the rooms, lingering in the alcove where Vincenzo was born on December 3, 1801. The room is now occupied by the harpsichord on which Bellini, returning from his Milanese successes, played in a festive mood the entire score of *Norma* in 1832, entertaining relatives and friends late into the night. The harp-

Bellini Museum in Catania.

sichord is open and a revolving stool is drawn close to a sheet full of notes: it looks as though someone just finished playing it. On a corner there is a worn down, eighteenth-century clavichord with keys that by now are without a voice. It belonged to his grandfather. Young Bellini practiced with yet untrained hands on it.

Not far from the clavichord there is another one, the one that Vincenzo junior bought for 530 francs, on which he wrote his signature. It was discovered by an antiquarian who then gave the heirloom to the museum.

The mementoes of Bellini's success in the great cities of Italy and abroad occupy a whole room: bills, prints, and letters recreate the climate of those years during the early nineteenth century when the young subject of the Kingdom of the two Sicilies came to be applauded at La Scala and Carcano theaters of Milan, at the Carlo Felice of Genova, at the Ducale of Parma, at the Fenice of Venice, and at the Italian theatre of Paris. By 1831, he had already composed and produced seven melodramas, among them the main works *La Sonnambula* and *Norma*, gaining a European reputation. The display cases hold miniatures and lithographs that reproduce the faces of the most famous Bellinian singers: the "Tre Giuditte"—-La Turina, la Pasta, la Crisi—Maria Malibran, Henriette Sontag, and Giovan Battista Rubini. Small objects catch the attention of those who visit: the notebooks with the musical notes, the musical scores of the youthful works that the future maestro signed "Vincenzo Bellini II" in order to distinguish himself from his grandfather, who was a pupil of Niccolò Piccinni and the author of oratories and sacred music. Inkwells, brooches, canes with silver handles, cups and miniatures, as well as two gold chains with a clock and a small good luck horn are kept in a display case beside precious, small carved boxes. Bellini was superstitious and his friend knew it: in Paris, Henrich Heine had some mischievous fun scaring him, and the musician would not stop casting spells every time he came across the German poet. One day, after having proved his abilities as a median by making a small table rise off the ground, Heine turned to the young maestro and said "You are a great genius, but you will expiate for your genius with a premature death. All the great geniuses die young, very young. You will die like Raffaello and Mozart…" An ill-boding prediction for Vincenzo Bellini stop living in Puteaux, near the French capital, on September 24, 1835. He did not live to see his thirty-fourth birthday.

The pathetic memento of a female admirer can be seen in another display case: The design of a five-chord lyre, one of which, the center one, is made out of a strand of the composer's blonde hair.

The maestro's own handwritten scores fill up numerous showcases. One can see the entire musical score of *I Capuleti e i Montecchi*, and the original of the first opera, *Adelson e Salvini*, performed in Naples in 1825 and applauded by Donizetti. The second edition of the *Puritani*, adapted for the voice of Maria Malibran; *Norma*, dedicated to Nicola Antonio Zingarelli, Bellini's teacher; *Il Pirata*; and *La Straniera* can be seen among other autographs. Among the youthful compositions, a *Tantum Ergo* composed at the age of nine (Bellini had written his first piece, *Gallus Cantavit*, for soprano, at the age of six, on a text of the canon Innocenzo Fulci, his Italian teacher). Of notable interest, specially for those who read music, are the pages of the large notebook of the "Daily Studies," in which Bellini scrupulously noted by hand musical themes as they came to him. Those that were used are crossed out, but there were many others that the composer, having died so prematurely, did not have time to use.

There are numerous portraits of Bellini, with his delicate features, clear gaze and blonde and curly hair: memoirs of an artist that the people from Catania called "the Swan," celebrated by the masses, admired by the elegant drawing rooms of Europe, idolized by the ladies. The images of triumph are overlapped by images of his death. The funeral mask is carefully laid down over a red velvet pillow inside a display case. In the fifties, Francesco Pastura, who was the director at the time, every time he had to remove it from the glass guard to facilitate the work of a photographer, he looked with sincere anguish at that face hollowed by suffering and pointed out that Bellini's eyes remained open at the end of his long agony, because the musician died alone and the wake did not take place for a long time. This circumstance calls to mind the air of suspicion that followed the musician's death.

The chronicles agree with the reports that, seduced by two adventurers, the English "couple" named Lewis, Vincenzo Bellini accepted their offer of hospitality in their villa in Puteaux, now a sector of the Parisian metropolis called Bellini. The musician lost all of his savings, amounting to thirty thousand francs, in the speculations of the host, receiving in exchange the favors of "Lady Lewis"—who was known by some as the "gay Mademoiselle Olivier"—and the tranquillity to compose *I Puritani*, the opera represented in Paris on January 24, 1835. But when the

Facade of the nineteenth century Bellini Theater in Catania.

sick man's condition grew grave, the Lewis couple vanished along with Doctor Montallegro, the physician who had written the bulletins on the course of the illness. These bulletins, all five of them, now at the Bellini museum, were tracked down by maestro Pastura in the workshop of a Milanese antiquary. The documents that make you relive the tragedy that overcame the composer at the highest point of his fame have a rare dramatic quality. The five small rectangles of yellowed paper are found in a shelving of the first sitting room, together with other documents pertaining to the musician's death, including the report of the autopsy conducted by the expert Dalmas by order of the King of France, Louis Philippe, who had heard rumors about the possible poisoning. Dalmas did not find any trace of poison, but he did find an intestinal inflammation complicated by an abscess to the liver that—he said—would have killed the young man in a few weeks.

Paris was shocked by the news of the unexpected death. The

Bellini's tomb in the Cathedral of Saint Agatha in Catania.

city, which had seen Bellini receive the Legion of Honor, took to mourning: the theatres closed their doors, and all festivities were suspended. Nine days later, a great crowd saw in silence the representation of *I Puritani* and the day after gave Bellini his last farewell. Rossini organized the funeral in the chapel of *Les Invalides* and Chopin composed the corpse. The Bellinian Museum preserves the documents of the funeral and on the transport of the body from Paris to Catania, which took place on September 1876, forty-one years after his death, and sixteen years after the end of the Bourbons' reign in Sicily. The Neapolitan authorities had blocked the transfer of Bellini's body to his native city that was asking for it, for fear that the homage to the illustrious son could give rise to manifestations of Italianism.

Together with the velvet covered coffin, the branches, the tapes, the wreaths that accompanied the transfer, there are the photographs of the solemn ceremony that took place in the Catania Cathedral, on the morning of September 24, 1876. The mausoleum, in the church that holds the relics of Saint Agatha, patron saint of the city, consists of a simple slab of marble on which the name Bellini is carved and by an allegory of the Genius of Melody. Almost always there is a fresh flower on the bare tomb.

A Refuge for Giovanni Verga

For him, his birthplace was a refuge and not a source of inspiration. His house was a vessel of memories. In his work, Giovanni Verga ignored the locales and people of Catania to focus his attention on the country people of Vizzini, where his family's properties were, and on the fishermen of the nearby Acitrezza. But in the city at the foot of lava-blackened Etna he gladly returned from travels and long stays in Florence and Milan, to enjoy the warmth of home, to abandon himself to his books and to his poetic ghosts, to the intimate and ever heavy correspondence with a few friends, and to the melancholy of old age.

The master of Verist literature was born and died in a house in the historic center of Catania, a respectable nineteenth century structure in Via Sant'Anna, whose door with round arch decorated with neoclassical ornaments is marked by the number 8. A memorial plaque on the second floor that the passerby can barely see reads: "Giovanni Verga, here he formed his world and concluded it, in the immortal power of art, 1840-1922." A second inscription below the first, placed there during the Fascist period, says, "The Municipality of Catania, in the year of the Great Sicilians, 1939-XVII". Via Sant'Anna joins Via Garibaldi and Via Vittorio Emanuele, two important arteries in the eighteenth century Catania rebuilt after the 1693 earthquake, within walking distance from Piazza Duomo, the Ursino Castle built by Frederick II of Swabia, the Roman Theater and the Baroque Via Crociferi. Via Sant'Anna seems now very narrow, because cars park permanently on both sides. However, as you cross the entrance gate, you take notice of the paved courtyard that once gave access to the stables and to the well designed, wide staircase with marble steps and elegant banisters, which underscores the economic solidity of the first owners.

Casa Verga is on the third floor, the "noble" floor. As you climb the stairs lit by large windows, the noises of the street wane and you cannot help thinking of the gentleman with large moustaches and a stern bearing, author of *I Malavoglia* and *Mastro Don Gesualdo*, who leaning against the railing, climbed those stairs countless times, with vigor or fatigue, depending on age and mood.

This house had been brought as a dowry to the "knight" Giovanni

Battista Catalano Verga, father of the writer, belonging to the younger branch of the Barons of Fontanabianca, by his wife Caterina Mauro, a young woman from an upper middle class family of Catania. Giovanni was born there on September 2, 1840 and there he spent a quiet childhood between his studies, which began at eleven in the school run by Antonino Abate, a scholar and patriot, and long vacations spent at home and in the countryside of Vizzini, close to that rural world of illiterates and humble folk that would be so dear to him. The library and the objects that he loved always remained in the Via Sant'Anna house, even when the writer stayed away from Catania for a long time. He returned there for good in 1894, except for some brief short trips to Rome and Milan. After the publication of *I Malavoglia* (1881) and *Mastro Don Gesualdo* (1889), he considered himself retired. He cultivated flowers on his balconies and only went out to stretch his legs. He would cross Via Garibaldi, enter Via Etnea and walk to the Circolo Unione at the Quattro Canti. The Club was a meeting place frequented by retired colonels, judges and nobles, more or less faded. At his death, on January 27, 1922, the house was left to his nephew, Giovannino Verga Patriarca, his brother Pietro's son. It was, in fact, the nephew who petitioned to have the apartment declared a national monument in 1940 and to have it remain as his uncle had left it, with its furniture, books, paintings and objects of the past.

He had almost a cult for those four walls and this made it possible to preserve the patrimony of the house even after the closing that occurred after Giovannino's death. The Verga house was purchased only in 1980 by the Sicilian Region, with the furniture, furnishings, books and papers, after a decree by the Department for Culture and Patrimony that made the funds available for the purchase and restoration required. The writer's birthplace was opened to the public in November 1984.

Not luxurious, but comfortable, the eight rooms have retained the King Umberto style that Verga wanted, offering a quiet and soothing atmosphere. The rooms reveal today the sobriety and taste of a man with stern manners who never wanted to create a family of his own, devoted to study and his commitments as a writer. After crossing the first room, in which are exhibited under glass photocopies of Verga's papers (the originals are in the University library), the visitor receives the first genuine emotion in the study that holds a heavy bookcase made of carved walnut and a solid table placed at the center of the room under a chandelier that probably for a long time was fueled with gas. As you gaze around the silent room, glimpsing the colored spines of the books, you see a bronze cast of a small woman's hand with slightly bent fingers, on the table covered with a green cloth. The cast represents the hand of the Piedmontese Countess, Dina Castellazzi di Sordevolo, whom Verga loved in the last thirty years of his life, a woman to whom he addressed over five hundred letters, which are now collected in a four-hundred page volume.

Here, among the more than two thousand volumes—many purchased by him, but most received as gifts and with a dedication—the writer paused to read and write and receive his friends.

This is the way, Ercole Patti, another Catanese writer, remembers him in his *Diario Siciliano*. He had had the good fortune, in 1920, to enter Verga's study in the company of writer Giuseppe Villaroel who had gone to visit the writer. Patti who "never tired of looking at him walking through Via Etnea and when he saw him in front of the Circolo Unione with his cane between his legs and his hands resting on the handle," on that occasion remained silent "as he good-naturedly spoke in Sicilian dialect, with the air of a provincial aristocrat," and could not "look away from the writer in a dark suit with his noble, white moustache ...."

Verga's library is representative of the tastes and interests of a writer who always admired the successes of the masters of naturalism, as evidenced by the presence on the bookshelves of works by Flaubert, Zola, De Maupassant, together with those of the great East Europeans Tolstoy, Dostoevsky, and Gorky. It is interesting to open up some of the books with dedications in them, following the indication in the library catalog compiled by the Book Patrimony Office. The one written by his friend Luigi Capuana, dated December 21, 1907 on the title page of his story *Cardello* is a little odd, but humorous. The dedication says: "To the well-born and diligent young pup, Giovanni Verga, who so far has earned ten *cum laude* for his cute, little compositions and especially those entitled V*ita dei campi, Novelle Rusticane, I Malavoglia* and *Mastro don Gesualdo*, to inspire him not to give in to laziness..."

The dedication full of admiration by the prophet of Futurism, Filippo Tommaso Marinetti (1912) is also surprising, as is the one from Dino Campana (1914). The latter, in a copy of his *Orphic Songs*, defined Verga "the greatest Italian of today." Giuseppe A. Borgese called Verga a "maestro"; for Lucio d'Ambra, he was "Teacher of all"; and Guido da Verona defined him, "great, good, and alone."

In the study, the ugly, vaguely funereal plaque donated by the city of Catania in 1920 for the writer's 80 birthday is preserved. It praises the writer for his "luminous interpretation and representation of the Sicilian soul, supreme novelist of the New Italy." Verga did not go to receive the plaque and did not take part in the festivities in his honor held in the golden space of the Bellini theatre. He sent his friend Federico De Roberto to represent him. Luigi Pirandello delivered a noble and enlightened essay and Dario Niccodemi, brought greetings from the Writers Association to the great Catanese writer. However, that same evening Verga went to see Pirandello to say: "Forgive me, I owe you all my gratitude, but from official Italy I do not want any honors." He obstinately considered himself a victim of injustices, and on his eightieth birthday he did not appreciate being appointed Senator for life by the King with a telegram sent to him by the Prime Minister, Giovanni Giolitti. As a monarchical and a Crispi follower, he answered with a curt telegram whose content he shared proudly with his brother Mario. His nephew Giovannino, who lived with his uncle until 1922 after the death of his father in 1903, recalled that on receiving the news of his nomination to Senator for life, Verga had a bitter consideration to make: "They are too late, now that I'm old I cannot even use the free rail tickets." But he actually did use the free train tickets that senators had the right to, to go to Rome for the swearing in ceremony, for his family members and also for the Countess of Sordevolo, as indicated by a letter dated December 28, 1921.

Giovanni Verga in a well-known period photo.

With a thin and bloodless face, Verga was laid out in his study on a bier on a rainy day in January 1922, wearing his new tails on which stood out the cross of the Civil Order of Savoy, between laurel branches lying along the bookcases. A few days earlier, returning from the usual visit to the Union Club, he had fallen heavily to the ground after suffering a stroke, and had never regained consciousness. The room past his study is the bedroom where Giovanni Verga died. There is still the bare bed, of painted iron, on which the writer lay wheezing one day and one night, assisted by Federico De Roberto in tears and the women of the house.

Almost as if to testify that everything remains as it was at the time of the death of the writer, there paintings over the fireplace sre still there sd are the furniture and the large, dark walnut armoire with the mirror. His shiny hat is still in the hat box, and three ceremonial suits, large and heavy overcoats of black cloth under which you can see other clothes, hang in the armoire. What you see from the window of this room lightens the image: on the other side of the street stands the Convent of the Poor Clares where his mother had studied too. Leaning through the window, the young Verga could perhaps have made eye contact with some young convert. It's possible that from such an emotion emerged the first idea of writing the *Storia di una Capinera* that was later published in Milan in 1871.

Proceeding farther in you enter the sober dining room. And here there is a piece of furniture that looks like a cupboard, but is, in reality, a well hidden service elevator. Verga notified the cook on the upper floor that dinner could be served by ringing an electric bell. You have to open a cabinet door to discover the little secret, but it is precisely through such family gadgets, this domestic device of a well-to-do home, that gives the tone of a tranquil bourgeois residence, a sense of a safe haven, to the birthplace of Giovanni Verga.

The Legend of "Nick the Fish"

The legend of Nick the Fish (*Colapesce*) is a story of altruism, generosity, devotion, obedience, and sacrifice: it is a myth recounted by reporters, historians, essayists, philosophers, in Latin and in ancient Italian, in Spanish, French and English, with an infinity of variants since the Middle Ages in Sicily and in the Mediterranean area. The myth has been embraced by scholars and travelers, storytellers and poets, Provencal troubadours and writers of folklore of the twentieth century.

In the best known version, the fable narrates about the son of a fisherman from Messina, named Nicola, but known as Cola, and nicknamed Colapesce (Nick Fish) for his swimming ability. When he surfaced from his numerous dives in the sea, he would tell of the wonders that he had seen in the depths and once he even came to the surface with a treasure. His fame reached the King of Sicily, the Emperor Frederick II, who decided to put him to the test. The Monarch and his court thus went out to sea in a large boat. As a first test, the King threw a cup into the sea and immediately Colapesce recovered it. The King then threw his crown into the water in a place known for its strong currents, and Colapesce again succeeded in the challenge. For the third time the powerful lord tested the swimmer by throwing his precious ring in a deeper part of sea, and once more, Colapesce generously dived into the sea's depths, but time passed and Colapesce never came back to the surface.

According to the popular story, as he dived into the depths of the sea that no one had explored before, Colapesce had seen how Sicily rested on three columns. One of the columns was dangerously worn out, and he decided therefore to stay underwater, to support the column with his arms to prevent the island from sinking. And today, Colapesce is still at the bottom of the sea, continuing his noble mission.

The most accomplished literary comparison was made by Miguel de Cervantes, who took part in the Battle of Lepanto in 1571 and was treated for his wounds in the large hospital of Messina. Talking with the other patients, he probably heard the tale of Colapesce, and as he listed the qualities that an Errant Knight must possess in the pages of his *Don Quijote,* he remembered the Sicilian legend. He wrote that the Knight "Must be an expert in justice and must know the laws of distributive and commutative justice, he must be a theologian, above all a botanist so he can recognize in the uninhabited countryside and deserts the herbs that have the virtue to heal wounds. I say also that he must know how to swim as well as people say that Pesce-Cola did."

Friar Salimbene de Adam from Parma, a historian and chronicler of the age of Frederick II who was a fierce enemy of the Emperor, so much so that he called him "a heretic and an Epicurean" also related the story of Colapesce in his *Cronica*—in fact, he was one of the first—and he underlined the cruelty of the Sicilian lord. In the account he handed down to us, Frederick II, who was on board a ship at anchor in the Straits in 1233, wanting to test the fisherman from Messina, repeatedly forced him to go down to the bottom of the sea to bring to the surface a gold cup thrown, on purpose, into an area where whirlpools made ships founder. Cola dived in and recovered the cup. The amazed King then threw the cup in a deeper part of the sea and ordered the swimmer to go down for the second time. Cola resurfaced with the cup, and the Emperor, playing a cruel game, hurled it again in a more distant area. Once more, the fisherman plunged into the depths, but he never returned to the surface anymore.

In the sixteenth century, the historian Tommaso Fazello of Sciacca in his *History of Sicily*, did not let the occasion pass without addressing the tale of Colapesce and did so in a detailed account: "There lived in Messina, in living memory of our forefathers, a certain Cola Pesce, native of Catania, a man worthy of admiration for every generation, who abandoned human society and spent almost all of his life alone in the Strait of Messina, among the fish, to the point that he could not stay for long out of water. Thus people called him Fish. He disclosed many special and unknown secrets about the Strait that no Messinese could recount to me in spite of my attempt to discover them. He knew them well since as a marine animal he swam in those great depths and enormous watery spaces even when he was hindered by waters tossed by bad weather. When the people of Messina already looked at him as a true prodigy, in a particularly solemn day of festivities, in the presence of a large crowd, Frederick, King of Sicily, threw a gold dish into the sea...He didn't return among the living. People suspected that he slid into the cavernous hollow of the Strait and that he was crushed to death. If anyone then should question by what force of nature Cola could remain underwater for so long holding his breath, we have to believe that he had very spongy and concave lungs." Evidently Fazello, ignoring the myth of Colapesce, analyzed his behavior as though he were a real person.

In the eighteenth century the Marquis of Villabianca took up the legend, ascribing to Colapesce Catanese origins and referring not to Frederick II, but to King Alphonse of Aragon. He wrote inexplicably that there were two Colapesce and stated "the ability granted to him to swim in the sea was a punishment from heaven for the curse that his own mother placed on him."

Still in the eighteenth century, the scientist Lazzaro Spallanzani considered "the case narrated to us about a certain Cola from Messina who was given the name of Fish because he remained in water for a long time... facetious and tragic." Moreover, he stated that, after the daring swimmer's death in the sea, his body was found on the beach of Taormina. Still in the eighteenth century, the Scottish traveler Patrick Brydone, in the account of his stay in Sicily, took up the legend of Colapesce and wrote about some swimmers in Naples who were capable of diving fifty times and remaining under water three minutes without breathing. "But what was even more amazing," —the Scot added—"was the fact that Colapesce from Messina was able to stay several days under water without coming to the surface."

In more recent times, the ethnologist Giuseppe Pitrè devoted over one hundred and sixty pages in his essay on popular legends in Sicily to the story of Colapesce. He included an anthology of the literary versions of the ancient fable in his vast review. The physician-ethnologist from Palermo, known for his meticulous research, provided many names in his notes. Benedetto Croce, for his part, transferred the legend to Naples, using as points of departure precise historical and fabulous references. He wrote, in his *Neapolitan Stories and Legends*, about a "certain Niccolò Pesce who lived as a fish or almost, who was able to spend hours and days immersed in water, as though he were in his own element, without needing to rise to the surface to breathe." The philosopher continued adding other legendary elements: "Niccolò Pesce cunningly let himself be swallowed by some of the enormous fishes that were familiar to him and traveled in their body, until reaching the place he wanted go and then taking out an enormous knife he always carried with him, cut the belly of the fish and went out free to complete his investigations." Benedetto Croce wrote about "mysterious caves in the Castel dell'Ovo, that guarded handfuls of gems." He also related poetically the end of the intrepid swimmer: "Lifting his head, he saw above him clean and limpid water.

The water covered him as a marble tombstone. He realized he was in a space without water, empty, silent. It was impossible to seize the waves again, impossible to start moving. He was shut off in that place, there he ended his life."

The reference Carlo Levi made to it in *The clock* is remarkable. The text is an account of a trip in the heart of Italy in the first years of the postwar period. Departing from Rome, Levi reached Naples and there he stayed in the old market of the Vicaria that was so dear to Matilde Serrao and Salvatore Di Giacomo, "between quartered animals and entrails of every kind" where he walked in a "gigantic fleshy gut, the stomach of a great fish." Proceeding through alleyways and narrow streets, he came upon a rounded bas-relief, "in which a naked man was portrayed with his whole body covered with hair and scales. It was Colapesce, the mythological sailor who lives at the bottom of the sea with the sea monsters, scaly as he was himself; a male siren who beckons the other sailors to the depths, and devours them."

This is a different Colapesce from the one presented in the traditional Mediterranean tradition. But probably the author of *Christ stopped at Eboli* recalled Croce's characterizations who after relating the story of the Neapolitan Niccolò Pesce, paused to talk about what his coachman had told him about the "portrait of the swimmer carved in the bas-relief facing Vico Mezzocannone, walled in the corner house in the narrow alleys of the port." That bas-relief represented a hairy man, with a long knife in his right hand, which was the knife that Niccolò Pesce used to cut the belly of the fishes inside which he traveled. And you can still find him there in his old place today, even though everything was transformed by the building restorations of the city; but the bas-relief, removed from the condemned house, was placed on the wall of a newly built house in the empty space below a balcony on the second floor, with the old eighteenth century inscription under it.

This same eighteenth century marble headstone revealed the origins of the sculpture that was found while excavating the foundations for the piers in the port. It was a relic from a distant past if already at the end of the sixteenth century some scholars stated that it came from a small temple situated in the area of the port, representing the god Orion, a divinity invoked by sailors since the time of the Romans.

The Neapolitan philosopher was right in being shocked by the Colapesce sculpture because as a child he—as he wrote—wandered "with his imagination in the depth of the sea searching like the daring explorer did." We also should point out that in the Filomarino palace where he lived and died there is a Colapesce that is identical to the one present in the Vico Mezzocannone. It's a copy that elicited a sense of revulsion from Lidia Croce, the philosopher's daughter, whenever she saw it as a child on leaving the house.

The transcription of the legend done in the twentieth century belongs to Italo Calvino. The writer chose an imaginary dialogue:

"Cola! Cola! Come ashore! What are you doing?

"Cola, the King of Messina is here and wants to speak to you!"

[…]

Colapesce started swimming all around Sicily. After some time he returned. He related that at the bottom of the sea, he had seen mountains, valleys, caves and fishes of every species, but he had been afraid passing by the Lighthouse because he had not succeeded in finding the bottom.

[…]

Cola plunged underwater and stayed there for one whole day. Then he returned to the surface and told the King: "Messina is built on a rock and this rock rests on three columns: one is whole, one is splintered and the last one is broken."

O Messina, Messina,

One day you will be sorry!

And when the King threw the crown of the Kingdom in the sea, Colapesce, even though he was afraid, went down to the depths with a handful of lentils, saying: "If I succeed, I will resurface, but if you see the lentils resurfacing, I will never resurface."

The lentils surfaced. We are still waiting for Colapesce to return."

A great painter of our time, Renato Guttuso, painted the ancient myth in the one hundred and thirty square meters of the ceiling of the Vittorio Emanuele theater in Messina.

In 1985, he used light colors to represent, in a tear of blue, the classical Strait. However, there are neither Scylla nor Charybdis in this stretch of sea that was crossed by Homeric navigators. There are instead some splendid sirens with long hair, half women, half fish who amuse themselves playing with sea creatures on opposite shores. The water seemed agitated by the fins of the fish and by jumping dolphins. At the center of the composition, then, there is a naked and muscular man who dives with ease, abandoning himself to the liquid element.

Catania has dedicated a statue to the mythical hero. It is in the University square where Colapesce is portrayed in bronze holding the cup he just recovered from the sea in his hand.

Even the theater was seduced the solitary and daring fisherman.

Renato Guttuso's rendering of the Colapesce myth for a Messina theater.

Only two examples: in Milan he was brought to the stage at the dramatic theater for puppets of Onofrio Sanicola, and in Palermo he was represented in the Teatro delle Beffe, in a show of puppets, shadows and actors, under the direction of Ludovico Caldarera. The protagonist was the mysterious character of the fable, the timeless hero who comes to our own time from the bottom of human imagination.

The Marsala Adventure

The Marsala wine industry was born in the city from which it gets its name in 1773—a date commonly accepted—through circumstances that are legendary. At the heart of the mythical adventure is John Woodhouse, the son of a rich merchant from Liverpool. Around 1770, along with other Englishmen he would often land in Mazara del Vallo or in Marsala to purchase water softener, sumac, and almond and hazelnut shells, goods used in English industry. Part merchant, part adventurer, John Woodhouse loved Southern wines, and it seems that this love—together with the desire to get rich quickly—inspired him to send a substantial shipment of Marsala wine to England to commercialize and sell there.

Being a good merchant, he added a certain quantity of alcohol to each barrel, raising its alcohol content, to protect the wine from deteriorating during the long voyage. The time line—a mix of myth and reality —states that this took place in 1773 and that the ship was named "Elizabeth." There were seventy pipes on board (containing four hundred liters of wine each).

The Sicilian wine, reinforced with alcohol, had a sweet taste and was well received in England. The young merchant thus made the decision to create a viable industry in Marsala to produce a liquorous wine similar to the Sherry, Madeira and Porto wines. He began to work on something that destined to increase in importance as time passed. This enterprising Englishman made one of the most important deals of his pioneering enterprise when he signed a contract on March 19, 1800, with Admiral Horatio Nelson, who had been named Duke of Bronte the year before, to supply Marsala wine to the ships of the British fleet.

The other leading English figure who can be placed next to Woodhouse was Benjamin Ingham, a true commercial genius, according to the historian Raleigh Trevelyan. Ingham was 22 years old in 1806, the year in which he traveled to Palermo in the wake of the English contingent's arrival on the island, that in a few years would balloon to 17 thousand men. This massive presence of English troops—called, as you may remember, by Ferdinand IV to curb Napoleon's ambitions—attracted numerous merchants to move to the south of Italy. Benjamin Ingham, born in Yorkshire to a non-conformist religious family, was an entrepreneur of exceptional talents, capable of great determination in protecting his interests and in making his collaborators work with the same intensity. It took only one visit to Marsala, and a fleeting meeting with his compatriot Woodhouse, to make him realize that great profits could be made with wine. Thus he immediately sent word to his brother, Joshua in London (who had spent time in America) and sent him to the Iberian peninsula to study the methods used in Spain and Portugal to fortify the wine. Benjamin went to America himself and established an agency in Boston so as to have a specific reference point overseas.

Six years after his arrival in Palermo, Ingham had already set up a structure for the production of wine in Marsala a little more than a kilometer from Woodhouse farm. He started others in Castelvetrano, Campobello di Mazara, Balestrate and Vittoria. Drawing upon his brother's learning experiences in Spain and Portugal, Benjamin was able to produce a wine that was sweeter and more pleasing to the palate than the Woodhouse wine. The difference was due the use of the "solera" system, which consisted of producing a "perennial" wine, made of what was left in the half empty barrel after each drawing.

Around 1825, not having children of his own, Benjamin Ingham called from England his nephew Joseph Whitaker, his sister's son and about a year after that another Benjamin (Ben) Ingham, his brother's son, to involve them in his affairs. The senior Benjamin Ingham passed away suddenly in Palermo on March 4, 1861. But Vincenzo Florio, in a glorious moment of his industrial adventure, had already been in competition with the Englishmen for thirty years in the production of Marsala wine, beginning his activity in 1832.

The Woodhouse and Ingham-Whitaker industry was strong and prosperous and their product reached the farthest markets through a large fleet of ships they owned. The challenge posed by Florio was that of a solitary giant who possessed a managerial view of things and a drive that was truly visionary. He multiplied the number of existing tuna fishing plants, he gave impetus to the sulfur industry, he opened a foundry, developed the cultivation of citrus fruits, he foresaw the future of steam navigation and built a fleet comprised of 99 ships out at sea with one ship made of gold kept in his office (this gold ship was because of a law that prohibited civilians from having 100 ships in their fleet). Vincenzo Florio used the ships largely to export Marsala, and this contributed to the establish his industry and to make known a product that at his insistence had to be of high quality and long ageing.

Through the many events that have made up such a rich history, the Florio house, in 1929, merged with Woodhouse and with Ingham-Whitaker, absorbing the plants and becoming part of the Cinzano family. Since then the Florio company of Marsala not only kept the founder's name and logo—a lion drinking from a stream—but also maintained the methods of production. The plant, after overcoming numerous difficulties especially during World War II and after the First World War, has become one of the largest and most modern enological complexes of the region. The walls of the Florio plant in Marsala—which run for over one kilometer along the seashore road named after Vincenzo Florio—consist of an immense area: 105 thousand square meters of which a good 50 percent covered with structures.

There are eight cellars with high cement ceilings used to age the wine. In each cellar, millions of liters of Marsala of various vintages "sleep" in perennial semidarkness. Withdrawals are made with a precise pre-established rhythm, under strict controls.

Inside the Florio winery, a plaque commemorates remembers the visit by Garibaldi on July 19, 1862, two years after the victorious Sicilian campaign. In his honor, the sweet wine that the general liked was baptized "Garibaldi". The wine is packaged with a label that remembers the legendary leader of the Thousands.

Ulysses in Sicily

Sicily, despite being geographically positioned at the edge of continental Europe, redeems its isolation by remaining faithful to the myths of the classical world. In fact, the Mediterranean that bathes its shores has always brought the island close to the crucial events of ancient history, assigning it the role of protagonist in many events tied to the civilization of man. The insistence with which cultured men of different nationalities have made Sicily the heart of the most important poetic discourse of ancient times, the one that deals with Homer, *The Odyssey* and, of course, with Ulysses, must be seen from this vantage point.

We have to start with Samuel Butler of England, a restless writer who consistently attacked the conformity of Victorian society. His book *The Authoress of the Odyssey*, published in 1897, aroused disbelief and caused an uproar and Butler himself was ridiculed. In fact, Butler, after translating *The Odyssey* from its original text in Greek and completing a series of journeys through western Sicily, became convinced that *The Odyssey* had been written by a young Sicilian woman disguised as the character of Nausicaa, the daughter of King Alcinous of Scheria.

The writer searched for Scheria, the land of the Phaecians, in the British Admiralty archives and in the end, after finding in the Sicilian city the specifications described in the poem, he identified it as Trapani, The position of the rock of Malconsiglio, a short distance from Punta Ligny was a surprise for him. This rock, constantly pounded by the waves, if seen under certain light conditions, can look like a semi-submerged keel even today. To Butler, it looked like the ship of Alcinous, transformed into a rock by Neptune who was angry at the Phaecians for daring to help Ulysses to return home.

Butler was attacked and his book sold only two-hundred copies. He was grateful, however, to Trapani and its people who helped him in his field research. For this very reason, he made provisions in his will to donate the manuscript of his widely criticized book to the Trapani library. And so on May 6, 1903, his friend H. F. Jones handed the manuscript to the Mayor of Trapani. After more than sixty years, in 1968, Butler's book was translated into Italian and published by Celebes, a businessman from Trapani. It was translated by Giuseppe Barrabini, a scholar

Mosaic of Ulysses offering wine to the cyclops Poliphemus in Piazza Armerina.

native of Trapani who—as we will see later—has a precise role in our reconstruction.

In 1952, copies of a book written in English reached Sicilian newspapers and public libraries from distant New Zealand. The booklet, signed by Professor Lewis Greville Pocok, had an inviting title: *The Sicilian Origin of the Odyssey*. The book's thesis was simple and fascinating: "My discussion begins"—he wrote—"with Samuel Butler's discovery. The English author, who was born in 1835 and died in 1902, landed on Sicily during the last twenty years of the nineteenth century, and discovered that the Scheria of *The Odyssey* was the city of Trapani, in the northwestern part of Sicily. It was the first time in history that a scholar paid attention to the topographic details of *The Odyssey*. And the probability that his identification is correct is highly likely. And yet, many refused to believe what Butler wrote, so now it's my turn to say that Homer was an accurate topographer and that, not only Scheria, but other sites in *The Odyssey* are real."

While he did not accept everything that Butler claimed, Pocok agreed on one fundamental point: Trapani could only be the land of the Phaecians, the Homeric Scheria, adding the fact that the existence of a semi-sunken vessel-shaped rock (and in ancient times the similarities had to be almost perfect) in the sea that touches the city had inspired the whole episode of Ulysses' stay in the land of Alcinous and the beautiful Nausicaa.

This flourishing of studies urged the retired Trapanese artillery colonel, Vincenzo Barrabini (brother of Giuseppe, the translator of Butler's book), to continue researching. Thus he went farther than both Butler and Pocok. As he stated in his book *L'Odissea Rivelata (The Odyssey Revealed)*, published in Palermo in November 1967 by the Flaccovio publishing house, Barrabini found in the territory "evidence that corresponded in full to the poem." And he arrived at the conclusion that the journey of Ulysses in search of his homeland was nothing more than a circumnavigation of Sicily: leaving from Erice, going through the Straits of Messina, Taormina and Pantelleria, Homer's hero landed at Scheria, in the Trapani territory.

With the help of topography, he started adding more pieces to the mosaic started by Butler and continued by Pocok. Since then, the major controversy of a Homeric Sicily has become less faded, even though today it will be difficult to chip away at the framework of official criticism by which the Homeric sites correspond to those handed down by classical tradition, the same that we learned about sitting at our school desks.

The fact is that Barrabini's claim makes a lot of sense when he explains, for example, that Dulichio, the islet from which the Proci sailed to go to Ithaca, is Sicilian.

"Dulichio" argued Barrabini, "is a Greek word that means "long land" and between the islets of the lagoon of Marsala, there is an island officially named *Isola Longa* in Sicilian (Long Island), because it extends for six kilometers and is only one kilometer wide. If three thousand years ago people spoke Greek on this islet, the name couldn't be anything other than "Dulichio." And that Greek was the language spoken then is confirmed by the name "Carco," of classical origin, that currently identifies its southern portion.

Even the Cyclopes that Homer portrayed as monstrous creatures had to live, according to the conjectures of the Trapanese ex colonel, in the area of Trapani. In Pizzo Lungo, at the extreme southern end of Mount Erice, facing toward Trapani, there is the entrance of a cave that bears the traits described in the poem. The Cyclopes who came running to help when they heard the curses of Polyphemus blinded by Ulysses were, in actuality, peaceful people dedicated to sheep herding. The word "Cyclops", argues Barrabini, means "Moon face" and "round face." For proof—he concluded—one must only go to Trapani and observe the people of the nearby mountains who maintain their ancient features.

Though interesting in many ways, Barrabini's views may seem now somewhat farfetched, but, in fact ,the former Trapanese colonel was not the last one to dissect Homer's legend. In 1968, two German brothers, Armin and Hans Helmut Wolf, published the book *Der weg des Odysseus* ("The Path of Odysseus") in Tubingen, after a decade-long study. The two brothers, one an historian and the other an architect, followed a strictly geographic method.

Ulysses' route from Troy to Ithaca—the strongest point of their argument—is geographically traced on a sheet solely based on the nautical conditions provided by Homer himself. This journey leads us—according to the intuitions of the two Germans—from Troy to the Tunisian coast (for them, the land of the Lotus Eaters and the Cyclopes), passing by Malta, which they identified with the island of Aeolus, and continues along the southern and northern coastlines of Sicily.

The Wolf brothers identified on the island various locations described in Homer's poem: the port of the Lestrygones and the castle of Lamos in Erice; the island of Circe in Ustica; the temple of Hades and Persephone in Imera; the island of the Sirens in Punta Faro; Scylla and Charybdis in Messina; Calypso Island in Lipari. For the two Germans, Calabria was the land of the Phaecians.

When the thesis was presented in Sicily and more specifically in Palermo, it seemed revolutionary and much removed from the traditional interpretations of the Homeric places and from those of Butler, Pocok, and Barrabini.

There are more than seventy theories on the identification of Homeric locations. A geographic chart that shows all the locations according to the interpretations of a host of scholars would extend from the Persian Gulf to the island of Tenerife. But the topic requires some reflections on an ancient poetic text balanced between reality and myth, between a literary game and topographic research.

One thing is certain: Sicily is at the center of the Homeric tale and Ulysses in the poet's intentions knows the Mediterranean island. Ulysses, therefore, the hero of many adventures, valuable even for modern man, can be seen walking on Sicilian soil by reading only Homer's pages and relying on the classical interpretation.

Isn't Ulysses the veteran of the Trojan war who must confront the Cyclops Poliphemus in a dramatic moment of his adventure? And wasn't the myth of the Cyclopes born after finding gigantic fossils in Sicily that the ancient people didn't know how to identify? That single eye socket in the center of the huge skull was a typical sign of the presence of a "gigantic man" with one eye. This was the ancient people's conviction. But we have known for a long time that the large eye socket at the center of the cranium was only the nasal cavity of the little Sicilian elephant.

Here, therefore, is another piece of the puzzle to finally place Ulysses in Sicily. It is more proof in addition to those documented by Nat Scammacca who, along with his wife Nina, in 1986 patiently translated Pocok's book *The Sicilian Origin of the Odyssey* into Italian.

With all the reservations and subtle distinctions possible, we can give credit to Butler, Pocok, and especially to Barrabini. These tenacious scholars did not only rely on classical books, but also traveled many arduous and difficult roads and pathways seeking a fascinating truth that is more than just poetic. And this is what we can say in the conviction that the author of *The Odyssey* was thinking about Sicily, the island that he often called "Green Trinacria" and "Land of the Sun," to relate the episode in which the fabulous Kingdom of Alcinous and his beautiful daughter Nausicaa offered the shipwrecked Ulysses a perfect hospitality.

The Trinacria in England

A neon Trinacria shines at night in Trafalgar Square joining the chorus of lights in the famous London square. The Trinacria is on the building that houses the tourist office of the Isle of Man, whose symbol is made up of three moving legs bent at the knees, precisely like those of the Triskeles.

The second Trinacria, before you reach the Isle of Man, is on the Liverpool Pier, on the stern of the ferry boat that in four hours reaches the island that is sixteen kilometers wide and forty-eight kilometers long in the middle of the Irish Sea. The boat that has a sharp bow and highsides as befits a ship that must sail the stormy seas of the north even in winter, leaves the pier on time, followed by a large flock of large and noisy seagulls. The black buildings of Liverpool lose their contours in the fog that falls down on the steel-colored sea color.

A view of the Trinacria on flags in Douglas, the capital of the Isle of Man.

Sicily is far away, but the memory of her Mediterranean light shines on the yellow Trinacria painted on the lifeboats, printed on the label of drinks distributed on board, and engraved on the cutlery and the glasses of the ship's dining-room. But why is the Trinacria, this warm, living, luminous, and dynamic symbol of the sun, so far north? Who brought it here?

The first contact with Douglas does not reveal the mystery. The capital of the Isle of Man is a charming town of northern Europe, with a long wooden pier, and with low tides that at night retreat so much they expose the entire keels of the ships at anchor. In the endless winter nights, the fog horns howl at regular intervals to warn sailors of the dangers posed by the fog.

The Triskeles used as a decoration on a building.

This is a land of ancient conquests. The Scandinavians invaded it in 800 with intentions of plunder, but gradually fell in love with the island crowned by high mountains and green plateaus, and remained there. The ancient folk tales, stories that float in a light of legend, recall the meeting between the rough men of Scandinavia with the more gentle nature of the solitary island, located halfway between Ireland and England.

The historical period of the Isle of Man begins with the arrival on the island of the first Viking leader, Godred Crovan, in the year 1079. The *Chronicon Manniae*, compiled by monks of Rushen in the XII century, describes the events of this second Viking period on the island and speaks of the first king, King Orry, who is believed to be the Godred Crovan who came from Scandinavian regions. The son of King Orry, Olaf, who lived from 1113 to 1152, was the first ruler to be called "rex manniae et insularum." The latter's son, Godred II, became a vassal of Henry II of England and since then the island became a pawn in the war waged by the powerful neighbor against Scotland. But the Viking Kings continued to dominate the island; there were fourteen in all who

The one pound bill with the Triskeles.

shared power with fifteen bishops. During this entire period, the island was ruled by a Scandinavian system of government that has remained virtually unchanged until today.

The first Trinacria appeared on the Isle of Man at that time on a massive stone cross which is now in the center of a small country cemetery and on a large sword that king Olaf Godredson wielded to fight against the Moors. The British Museum experts state that the sword that is still used in official ceremonies, was forged in 1250. The stone cross goes back to the same period. In 1310, the Trinacria still appeared on the shield of Henry of Belmont, Lord of the island.

The official sources, books, and encyclopedias do not say how and why the three legs became the symbol of this northern land and the Douglas museum director is trying to find the key to the mystery. But perhaps the wings of a gentle poem recited to visitors by people gathering at the feet of the Medieval castles of Rushen and Peel can be more helpful than a dry documentation.

In the great silence of Fort Anne, broken only by the nervous flutter of gulls on the wide arc of the bay, I heard from the voice of a little, old lady the fascinating story. "It's simple" she replied when I insisted to know. "It was a Viking King who brought the Trinacria here. A monarch who had grown up on the Isle of Man met in Sicily the woman who quickened the beat of his warrior heart. She was a Sicilian princess. He married her and took her to Douglas where his duty required him to stay. But the princess languished in the mists of the north and she desperately longed for the sun. To console her, the King decided to adopt the Trinacria—the symbol of the Sicilian shining sun—as an emblem of the island instead of a Viking ship."

On the Isle of Man you can see the Trinacria everywhere. You will see it on paper money, on monuments, on office signs, on newspapers' headlines, matchboxes, stamps, and souvenirs. The island has an independent government and a parliament, even though geographically it is part of England. Elizabeth II who is Queen of the nearby islands, is only a Lord on the Isle of Man. Every year, reenacting a thousand-year old ceremony, the Deputies climb onto the top of an artificial hill built with the earth from all the districts of the island to read in the local language—quite different from English—the laws that the local legislators approved during the year. The people present at the solemn ceremony approve in silence, but they can publicly oppose them.

The Isle of Man had metal coins in the past, today there is only the paper Sterling issued by "The Isle of Man Bank Limited" that circulates on the island along with the "pound" with the portrait of Queen Elizabeth on it.

The inhabitants are proud of their independence, their very civilized institutions, their ancient monuments that represent a noble evidence of their past. They have a keen sense of hospitality and they are jealous of their Trinacria, the mysterious symbol of Mediterranean warmth that became a gift of love of a rough Nordic warrior when he was conquered by the beauty of a Sicilian princess.

The Vacation Island

Nine miles from Trapani, Favignana has 3400 inhabitants, plus another thousand if you include the inhabitants of Levanzo and Marettimo that are part of the same township. During the summer, however, especially during August, between fifty and sixty thousand vacationers crowd the island, attracted by the still uncontaminated waters, by the possibility of finding isolated places, and by the climate of dreamy summer leisure that pervades the area. They come from everywhere, finding lodging in hotels, private houses offered for summer rentals, *pensioni* and campsites. But the people who have a permanent summer home there arrive as well. They usually are from Palermo. That is why in the last decades, Favignana has become the Palermitans' vacation home.

Only the ones who are endowed with curiosity, out of the many that land on the island from ferries and hydrofoils, are able to discover the secrets of this very ancient island at the center of the Mediterranean. Rising form the sea like a gigantic butterfly, the island once was joined to Sicily. Abandoning the usual itineraries and the most frequented roads, you can discover the mysterious and fascinating side of the island. You can reach caves and deep cracks in the ground, deep ravines, precipices

The main square of Favignana.

edged with wild bushes and deep caves that sink to the center of the earth. These are the most eloquent signs of the changes caused by geological movements and by the endless pounding of the waves on the tufa rocks through millions of years. The action of the elements has uncovered fossil remains, carving out caves such as the Grotto of the Sheep and of the Ucceria—which date back to the same time period as the Grotto of the Genoese with its famous graffiti—and which were used as a place of refuge by primitive men. You can find evidence of this in the fragments of flint stones cut as knives that emerge from the sand even today and in Phoenician inscriptions and paleo-Christian burial niches. This unique scenario is made even more interesting by the fascinating presence of a stone called *calcarenite quaternaria*, a fine grain and compact stone, easy to carve which has been utilized in many ways through the ages. Think of the recently discovered funerary stones on the nearby island of Motya that were made with this stone. Originating from the sedimentation of sea water, the tufa stone was used intensively beginning in the eighteenth century. From the second half of the nineteenth century, the tufa stone of Favignana was used to decorate the façade of Baroque churches everywhere in Sicily, to build lordly residences such as the Villa Igiea of the Florio family in Palermo, and also the houses of poor people as well as industrial buildings.

The entrepreneurial family of the Florios left visible marks of their presence: the little villa built in 1867 was designed by Giuseppe Damiani Almeyda, who also built the Politeama Theatre in Palermo and the vast industrial complex for the canning of the tuna caught in nearby waters.

The little villa dominates the port. It served as the summer home of the Florios and their guests, but now it is used as the town hall. In the 1950s, there were still people who remembered the parade of elegant coaches brought from Palermo and the parties held in the elegant halls of the villa.

The industrial edifice built facing the western part of the port with the tufa stone of Favignana was a solid nineteenth century structure with impressive smoke chimneys and an iron gate decorated with the Florio emblem, still visible today: showing a lion bending down to drink from a stream. The tufa played an important part in the nineteenth and twentieth centuries. It was cut out of the caves in rectangular slabs and was delivered to the Sicilian coastline on large sailing boats.

The blocks were extracted in two ways: out of open air quarries or by digging deep tunnels. People worked in those tunnels with acetylene lamps under difficult conditions and with little oxygen.

While it is difficult and dangerous to visit the artificial caves, it is easy to visit the open-air quarries where one can still admire what remains since the tufa stone fell in disuse. Almost always in proximity to the sea, but also in the hinterland, you can see artificial bastions that reach down deep into lower ground that is used for cultivations or as animal pasture because it's protected from the wind. The steep walls are marked with horizontal lines: these are the marks left by the enormous hand saws handled with great expertise and effort to cut the tufa blocks that were called "cantoni". This is the sight offered to the visitor by the ghostly amphitheater of Calarossa with its tufa pinnacles similar to the spires of some fabulous castle. They form the background to the artificial galleries marked with old and new graffiti. The well protected bay which really begins at San Nicola point, ends at San Vituzzo point, an expanse of gray and sharp rocks that reaches down to the sea. It is a bay with transparent waters that was used by the Roman Consul Lutazio Catullus who in 214 BC fought against the Carthaginian fleet led by Annone. Hiding his fleet inside the bay, the Roman commander surprised his enemy and decimated his fleet. The battle ended with fifty ships sunk, 70 captured together with their crews and 10 thousand prisoners. It was known as the Battle of the Egadi Islands mentioned by Polibius who did not write about the victims. Nevertheless, the blood of all the fallen must have turned the water of the bay red if the name of Red Bay remained for that place of ambush.

In Calarossa, as well as in other rocky shores made of tufa, you can find the sculptures of the most extraordinary naïf artist in the Egadi islands: Rosario Santamaria, known to the tourists as Zu Sarinu. Santamaria, who died in 1992 at eighty years of age, was an illiterate stone carver who had imagination and a great artistic talent. Thanks to these qualities he was able to sculpt heads of tufa stone marked by touches of irony that reproduced approximately his own features, with his characteristic sunken cheeks and enormous nose. He placed many of his heads on top of pilasters of solitary gates, on top of walled dividers and on house facades. A silent population of heads continues to live on Favignana even after his passing. Zu Sarinu was so popular that one day Salvatore Fiume, a guest on the island took his canvas and his brushes and painted a portrait of his "colleague." The sculpted heads in

Calarossa are the work of Santamaria, but there are many other tangible testimonials that he placed in solitary rocky points of Favignana, even those that are more inaccessible except to him who knew how to reach them. There is also a strange bas-relief whose age cannot be ascertained that shows a face carved inside a circle, like an icon. It was not created by Santamaria, but by one of his pupils, Antonino Campo. Santamaria taught sculpture to several young people of talent and Campo may be considered his direct continuator. Nature and art, therefore, forming a fantastic intermingling, combine to lyrically express the magic of the surreal landscape of Favignana.

In Pirandello's Homes

I am in Luigi Pirandello's home on Via Bosi in Rome, together with the writer's grandson, attorney Pierluigi Pirandello, son of Fausto, the painter. It is a rare occasion in an ordinary day at a quiet time in the morning, undisturbed by the few cars that pass by. At number 14 there's the gated entrance of the Qatar Embassy. On the opposite side of the street, at number 15, there is the gate that's the entrance to the villa where on the second floor, the Sicilian playwright lived.

My thought recalls the distant day of December 10, 1936 when the Nobel Prize winner passed away, exactly two years after he received that prestigious award in Stockholm, and the funeral that took place the day after, as the writer as prescribed in his testament, using "a lowly carriage, a carriage used by poor people." The French journalist Henry Mercadier, as told by Enzo Lauretta in his *Pirandello fuori chiave*, saw that carriage "appear in Via Bosio in the first hours of the foggy morning in Rome and saw it roll down desolately alone through via Torlonia at a slow trot of the unknowing horse…The last carriage was coming to

Pirandello's desk with a photo of Marta Abba and the typewriter used by the playwright.

collect Pirandello and lead him toward immortality."

A large marble slab on the façade of the building of the gate dedicated by the city commemorates "The novelist, short story writer, poet, creator of a new theater who expressed the suffered travails and dramatic restlessness of his age through imperishable pages." The house is today the headquarters of the Institute of Pirandellian Studies presided by Sandro D'amico, son of the great theatrical critic, Silvio. The ground floor is occupied by the Central Metrical Office of the Ministry for Industry, Business and Artisanship and on the second floor by the Metrology Laboratory. Pirandello probably would have used these two technical departments with important functions as scenarios for some characters of his plays, if they had been there in his lifetime.

Uncle Stefano lived on the ground floor, says Pierluigi, and there his grandfather went to eat. A window in the stairs opens onto the courtyard bordered with hedges separating the building from the street. Looking at the courtyard, Pierluigi recalled how Pirandello loved big Lancia automobiles and that a yellow one often parked there. There is no elevator in the building, even now. Pirandello had to climb sixty steps to reach his apartment and he faced the staircase several times a day. The house was not large, but it was bright. It had a terrace and living room studio that was large compared to the other rooms, especially the one where he slept. It was very small and was left exactly as it was after his death, with its little bed with yellow brass, the crucifix at the head and a night table with a nineteenth century lamp.

This is the first strong impression you get after crossing the threshold of the house, through the secretarial office of the Institute. But it's the presence of Pierluigi, the direct heir of the writer, that provides a magical sense to the visit. And naturally it's derived also from the living room studio that you traverse in respectful silence not to disturb the climate of the space, not to upset the Pirandellian ghosts that seem to still float between the library, the large desk and the square little table carved in black wood on which rests the typewriter Pirandello used.

There are mementoes everywhere. The ones on the writer's work desk offer witness and documentation of his genus. Approaching them to try to read them you get the feeling that you are violating the secrets of the literary enterprise of a genius, but you can't help but notice the 1936 calendar still opened on the month of December. One of the grandchildren wrote on the page of December 7: "Grandfather is in bed." On the page of December 9, a Wednesday: "Still in bed." From December 9, it skips to the 11: The day of the 10 which perhaps contained the notation of his death is missing. It has vanished inexplicably.

A dossier, at the center of the desk, contains the proofs for his *Il berretto a sonagli* with his meticulous corrections. The word "Fiorica" lacks an accent mark. Pirandello wanted it written "Fioríca". "Fifi" was corrected as "Fifí".

There is a photo of the very young Marta Abba looking like a school girl, smiling widely and showing her teeth. She was the student and actress whom Pirandello surrounded with deep, intellectual love, a tormented feeling that induced him to write in 1931, in one of the 560 letters addressed to her: "The poor Maestro far away (that is what she called him always using the polite form of address for him) is accustomed to waiting, to receiving only rare replies to his letters, one reply for every five of my letters." This letter is from the year before: "I am writing to you: this is the only parenthesis of real living in my whole day." On the desk there is a silver box given to him by Gabriele D'Annunzio, whose "pompous opulence" Pirandello decried. Then on a bulletin board the colorful dossier from the "Svenka Akademien," representing the official certificate of the Nobel Prize awarded in 1934 on the first ballot, over 28 candidates among whom Eugene O'Neill.

The paintings on the wall are the work of his son Fausto, "The Solitary Painter of Italy," who was able to find a way to express his own individuality in spite of being crushed by the weight of his father's name. The 1929 painting "Bagnanti" which has a solid structure is hung together with "Crocifissione" from 1934. There is also a tender portrait of his sister, Lietta, painted in 1931 wearing gloves and a little black hat.

In the bookcases, in spite of the nets used to seal them, you can see book covers covered with pleasing geometric patterns in color. They were probably drawn by Pirandello as he pondered the endless plots of his novels and theatre: ten thousand pages written in fifty of the sixty nine years of his life that have influenced the course of literature and drama of our time in the whole world. As the writer consciously declared, it was an opus that "once passions waned, (I hope) that it live before man in its nakedness and wholeness, clear as it was in my spirit when I regarded it complete and perfect for a moment."

Before leaving Casa Pirandello, his grandson who is a tactful and passionate enthusiast of his grandfather's and father's memories, granted me a last wish. He allowed the removal of the very formal and highly decorated uniform as a member of the Italian Academy from the closet and let me photograph it. It was a very emotional moment.

A theater in Pirandello's house. Pierluigi Pirandello had it built together with his young friend, the architect Giancarlo Palombi. He had dreamed of this initiative for a long time and it was finally completed in the house where the painter Fausto Pirandello lived from 1954 to his death in 1975 at the age of 76. It is a short distance from Piazza del Popolo and the lazy flowing Tiber.

Pierluigi Pirandello, a civil lawyer, is a tall man with graying hair who bears a striking resemblance to the other members of the Pirandello family. He is very open to all and has a rare capacity for opening up to his friends and welcoming them into his home together with his wife. He is, however, an extremely reserved person who does not like to show off. The quiet tone of his words, uttered with many pauses, fully reveals his personality.

He said that he had nurtured the idea of building "A little theater for his friends"—that's what he called it—for a long time, and postponed it because of his professional obligations.

Why build a little stage within the walls of his house? Pierluigi Pirandello does not hesitate in answering: "I have great affection for the theater which certainly was in the family genes. I tried to do something useful for culture and also because I liked doing it. I owe a lot to friends such as the director Luigi Petrini who offered their collaboration. There was also another motivation: I hoped to pay back for some of the wrongs done to playwrights. Often access to a theater is not easy. I hope to discover some new talents. Perhaps I am being too ambitious, at any rate, I am willing to try."

"The Little Theater for My Friends" was created in September 1996. Naturally, the stage is not very large, but it is harmonious. It has an appropriate backdrop toward the back and beautiful red velvet curtain chosen by Pierluigi's wife, Mrs. Giovanna Carlino Pirandello, a Sicilian woman from Ribera, an intellectual who is affectionately supportive of her husband's cultural initiatives. The theater can accommodate about seventy people and some more standing. Luigi Petrini was the director who inaugurated the theater with the play *La mansardina*, a work by Francesco Paolini, "a talented artist who has not received the recognition he certainly deserves," as the host commented. In this period, the same Luigi

Petrini, together with a troupe of actors who work well with each other (they are also dubbers), are rehearsing Shakespeare's *Othello*, making the tragic story of the Moorish captain, Desdemona and the servant Iago echo along the Tiber River.

What about the viewing public? The attorney says: "This is a homebound theater. For this reason, only those who live nearby are invited, family friends, the friends of the authors, actors, and the director."

The rehearsal is on. With a respect for the theater, its rituals and its ghosts that borders on the religious, Pierluigi Pirandello shows how to do it, crossing the hall that is dominated by an exceptional object with remarkable documentary and affective values: on the old painting stand there is an unfinished painting by the master. He invites the guests in the other rooms, into the dining room, the living room. This way the guests have the clear sensation of crossing the threshold of a magic realm known through the mediation of books and of literary testimonials. Indeed, through a third generation descendant, the stories of his father Fausto and his grandfather Luigi come alive. Besides, Pierluigi himself admitted, "My passion for the theater sometimes makes me neglect my professional activities and at times my clients complain. But I have always met my obligation to defend the weak, even though I realize that I am devoting my time to my father and grandfather. His grandfather painted Pierluigi's portrait in 1936 when the grandson, who was born in Paris in 1928 during his father's stay in the French capital, was eight years old. Today the portrait is displayed in the dining room. In the canvas, the boy is portrayed with his elbows on the arm rests of a little arm chair. His face is turned to the left in a pose that must have pleased his grandfather so much that he wanted to portray it in an oil painting.

Art, whether expressed through the use of the pen or with a paint brush, was alive in the Pirandello family. Art critic Giuseppe Appella, presenting about one hundred of Fausto's paintings in Macerata in 1990, traced parallels between Luigi's teachings and Fausto's: "The characters created by Luigi and Fausto are easily identifiable; they have recognizable and straightforward attitudes that are maintained in the remaining portion of the painting and of the short story. The former are pictorial as the latter are descriptive."

In the Roman house where the little theater is, there breathes an unmistakable Pirandellian atmosphere.

The host talks about his father, a solitary man who had his first

Pierluigi Pirandello in his little theater.

big exhibition only after his death. He recalls, "'Art does not pay,' my father used to say. For many years he lived on money that grandfather gave him. He advised me not to become a painter because I would starve to death. That is why I got a law degree and I embraced the profession." Nevertheless, he relates with admiration the story of his father's life in the Paris at the end of the '20s and the beginning of the '30s. "There he established friendships with the Italian group, such as Severini, De Chirico, Savinio. He was fascinated by Picasso, charmed by Matisse and curious about Braque."

We talked about his grandfather also who died when Pierluigi was still young and we talked about his father next to whom he lived for a long time. At a certain point, we could no longer hear the actors' voices. The rehearsal had ended and we could meet the protagonists of the "Little Theater for Friends."

A Hotel Symbol

There is a subtle magic in the elements of the landscape of Taormina. From the garden of the San Domenico Palace Hotel, a terrace overlooking the Ionian Sea, you can see a green valley and a long arc of the coastline until it meets the smoking immensity of Mt. Etna, at times covered with clouds, at other times sharp and clear against the clean, blue sky. In winter, the view is even more spectacular because in the green space of the valley the first flowers are blossoming while the volcano remains covered with snow. But it is the well kept garden of the San Domenico, characterized by a silence that seems surreal, that puts the guests in touch with nature. The thick tunnel of ivy, the hibiscus, the cacti, the exotic kapok, the agave flowers reaching towards the sky, the oranges that hang from the trees, make it a happy Eden. In addition, the garden emanates seductive perfumes. The lavender borders, planted here and in the cloisters by a talented horticulturist, emanate a light and delicate perfume that caresses and offers solace, creating an air of indefinable well being: a caress for the olfactory glands.

These are some of the reasons that through the course of the years have contributed to the growth of a high class tourism that focuses on the natural and artistic beauties of the ancient Tauromenion, the quiet and the relaxation that are made possible not only by the echoes of the classical period, but also by the villas placed on its slopes and often hidden by the exuberant vegetation. The men from the north are captivated by a sort of enchantment that keeps them from abandoning the terrace on Mt. Tauro on which Taormina sits like a goddess on Greek Olympus. Those who leave conserve a memory linked to an image, the face of a woman, a happiness achieved or lost. That is the case of the unknown English traveler who characterized himself as "the Nomad" who many years ago placed at the entrance of the San Domenico garden a little bronze plaque to remember something that is personal and universal at the same time. "Here, in this sunbathed garden, she relaxed under the shade of trees that welcomed her, offering her a refuge. In this splendid garden overlooking the Ionian Sea, she planted a tree: the tree of remembrance. In this tranquil garden flowers blossom and as they bloom they tell a love story during the day and in the quiet of the night. With their perfume, the flowers speak of her who loved them so much."

Romanticism of another era? The fact that the plaque was walled in by someone who was a guest of the San Domenico, the famous monastery-hotel, the best known in Taormina and the world, makes you think of the sortilege that a stay there can engender. The wide corridors painted in white that for centuries echoed only the monks' silent steps and heard the chants of the community gathered in prayer, the rooms that were used as cloistered cells, the paintings and the statues of saints, the stalls of the choir, speak of a monastic life.

The San Domenico since when it was converted into a luxury hotel for demanding guests from all over the world (1896) has evoked fascination. In the golden register of the monastery-hotel—a parchment paper book with gold decorations that is kept in the safe—there is the story of the interest that Taormina has exercised on reigning monarchs and famous personalities of the world of politics, art, music, diplomacy, and the theater. This extraordinary repertoire of illustrious signatures was begun in the winter of 1905 on the occasion of the arrival of Germany's Kaiser, who inaugurated the register by donating a picture of himself taken in the hotel's garden covered with snow (a truly unusual event for Taormina). In 1913, the Grand Duke of Russia, Paul, and Countess Hoenfelsen signed it, as did French writer Anatole France. Amedeo of Savoy left a mark of his presence there in 1922 and at the same time the Russian biologist, Serge Volonoff, famous for his experiments on "rejuvenation". In 1925, Guglielmo Marconi stayed at the San Domenico and on the register under his signature wrote the note "hoping to return". Two years later a crowned head, Alphonse XIII, rested on a pillow of the hotel. On leaving, the King wrote only "Alfonso" with an embellished A. In 1928, Luigi Pirandello signed the register and in 1937 the gloomy Himmler. In the same year, the genius of central European music, Richard Strauss signed it and Rodolfo Graziani signed it twice, in 1938 and in 1953, characterizing himself as "a simple Italian soldier."

There are many names and signatures, some famous, others less: Rodolfo Farinacci (1939) Alcide De Gasperi (1948) King Farouk (1950), the American Ambassador to Italy, Clare Boothe Luce (1954). The French writer Roger Peyrefitte who wrote seventeen novels in Taormina, signed in 1991, recalling his stay in 1954 marked by his meeting with Thomas Mann in the hall of the hotel. There are many signatures that cannot be deciphered or counted, but we can still name a few more. In the 1960s Willy Brandt, the King of Sweden and Nelson Rockefeller signed the gold register. Rockefeller expressed this lapidary judgment: "Delightful". In 1979, painter Renato Guttuso signed his name next to a dove drawn with the same pen and in 1938 playwright Tennessee Williams signed. The great Eduardo De Filippo left his spiritual testament to his theater colleagues: "I beg you: love each other, as the public loves you. This is the secret for success." François Mitterand signed in 1989, Gerald Ford in 1993, and Jorge Amado in 1995, appending this note to his signature: "There is no other hotel like this."

But some illustrious men sometimes distracted by their numerous worldly engagements, did not leave a trace of their stay in the golden register. Almost all the Hollywood stars who in the sixties stayed at the San Domenico when the International Cinema Awards were held in Taormina, forgot to sign the register. But at that time, the entire Olympus of world cinema stayed at the San Domenico, slept in the ancient cells of the monks, walked along the garden and in the cloisters. The many photos shot then show Susan Hayworth, Cary Grant, Rex Harrison, Marlene Dietrich, Joan Crawford and Charleton Heston, Anthony Perkins and Ingrid Bergman, Audrey Hepburn and Sofia Loren, not to mention many other figures connected with the cinema industry.

The history of the San Domenico records also the interest that the cinema had for its extraordinary spaces. On a New Year's Eve (in the sixties), director Michelangelo Antonioni, who had been in the hotel for some days with Monica Vitti, noticed that a large hall that had been emptied for a party, placing the furniture all in one corner, evoked a desperate feeling of abandonment. He asked then that the hall be left exactly like that for one day and he used it to shoot the last scene of the movie *L'avventura*. In the same film you can see the strangest painting of the rich San Domenico collection: it portrays a young woman as she breast feeds an old man. The painting is displayed in the great hall and it immediately attracts the guests' attention.

The transformation of the building into a hotel is interesting. The church and the monastery were built in the XV century by a noble Catanese, the Dominican friar Damiano Rosso, belonging to the princely family of Rosso of Hauteville. In 1430, the friar bequeathed all his belongings to the monastery, but with a clause that came to be known only four centuries later in 1866 under curious circumstances. It was the year when all ecclesiastical possessions were to be turned over to the State and, of course, the Italian functionary charged with taking possession of the building showed up at the San Domenico. The representative of the Italian State awkwardly tried to wrest the keys from the hands of the last monk remaining within the ancient walls, friar Vincenzo Bottari Cacciola. The outraged Dominican (the episode is told on the tombstone of the friar in Taormina's cemetery) "took his revenge by revealing to the noble heirs of Damiano Rosso a secret and unknown testament." A parchment document that had remained secret until then stated that the monastery would revert to the heirs if the friars abandoned it. So it was that the princes of Cerami, heirs to Rosso of Hauteville, took possession of the building, which was then transformed into a hotel.

Another curious thing is the existence of an apartment named "Truman," decorated with Chinese lacquers and splendid brass beds. The suite had been prepared for the American President at a time when it seemed certain that he would come. But he never came, and the suite remained and it is open to guests in its more comfortable and sober look.

The gardens of the San Domenico.

The San Domenico, in the final analysis, is a high class hotel equipped to satisfy the needs of a most refined international clientele. For this reason, besides offering the spaciousness of its vast garden and private terraces, the warmth of the hall decorated with precious antique furniture and works of art, it focuses on the quality of the services it offers, its international cuisine, and a wine cellar stocked with great vintage wines.

In summer evenings, when the main avenue of Taormina is full of sleepless tourists, the cloisters of the hotel monastery illuminated with lights that filter through the leaves, become a cool, quiet and welcoming oasis. All you need to feel satisfied after a day of sun, sea, and entertainment, is to hear the sound of a mandolin expertly played by someone who knows and plays old and ever popular tunes of the international repertoire, in the best musical tradition of Taormina.

Sciascia: a Destiny

The title of this chapter was suggested by a sentence uttered by Claude Ambroise, professor of Italian language and literature at the University of Grenoble whom Leonardo Sciascia called "my critic" in an often cited page of his diary-confession, *Nero su nero*, written in 1979. This is what he wrote: "Among my critics, all of a sudden my critic emerged, the critic that became my critic out of perseverance and passion."

Ambroise, who was also the editor of the three volume *opera omnia* of the Racalmuto writer published by Bompiani between 1987 and 1989, told me the following when I interviewed him right after Sciascia's death: "By now Sciascia has become for us a destiny of our life because his life became a destiny."

This premise seemed indispensable to me because for me, too, Sciascia represented a "destiny" from the time I had the good fortune of meeting him at the beginning of 1963. I was in Palermo in the Flaccovio bookstore perusing and leafing through some of the new books placed on a table. A short man properly dressed in a gray suit with shirt and tie was doing the same thing facing the opposite table. He was Leonardo Sciascia whose first books I had read with interest and who was the object of articles in the national press. But I had never met him.

The bookstore owner and editor, Salvatore Fausto Flaccovio passed between us and slowing down his quick-paced *Bersagliere* walk, stopped to say hello, jovial as always, to his two friends. He introduced me to Sciascia who had read in the third page of the *Giornale di Sicilia* one of my articles on the Sicily of the eighteenth century which had

Leonardo Sciascia posing for the author.

become a subject of interest for the public following the publication of Sciascia's novel *Il Consiglio d'Egitto (The Egyptian Council)*, and the theatrical piece by Luchino Visconti *Il diavolo in giardino (The Devil in the Garden)* that was playing in Palermo at the time. The meeting quickly provided me with a measure of Sciascia's personality and his stature as a writer.

He had read the article and thanked me for all the space given to his book and its placement of the page adding that he had appreciated the critical comments that then I had written with a bit of youthful arrogance, as I realize now. I was surprised and flattered also because the writer completed his remarks by saying that he did not like literary critics who lavish praises without reservation and that he preferred by far polemical statements and even possible challenges.

We exchanged addresses and from Caltanissetta—where he lived before moving for good with his wife and two daughters to Palermo—He invited me by telegram to lunch in a restaurant in the center of town. It became a habit of his to invite friends for lunch when he came to Palermo. There were no more than four or five people at a time and among the other guests I remember only Flaccovio, his editor.

In 1964, I reviewed *Death of the Inquisitor* for the *Giornale di Sicilia*, an essay published that year on the dramatic story of Diego La Mattina, the monk from Racalmuto who in 1657 killed the inquisitor Juan Lope de Cisneros in the Palermitan prison of the Holy Inquisition. He was burned at the stake the following year.

That was also the year that I discovered some cells of the Holy Office—in the 14th century palace of the Chiaramonte family, known as the Steri, which had been used to hold the Tribunal's archives. Owing to his interest in the inquisition and the main character of his essay on Diego La Mattina, Sciascia was very moved by this event which I made known through the press. We exchanged letters and perhaps even some phone calls and it happened that we visited, in a clandestine way, the cells of the Steri Palace to survey the sight. This intellectual adventure had a development because following our visits the cells were arbitrarily demolished to Sciascia's utter indignation. The whole matter was told in the preface to his book *Graffiti e disegni dei prigionieri dell'inquisizione (Graffiti and Drawings by the Prisoners of the Inquisition)*, published by Sellerio in 1977. I wrote about it too in the appendix notes to the book by Giuseppe Pitrè and Leonardo Sciascia, *Urla senza suono (Screams Without a Sound)*, published by the same editor Sellerio in the series "La memoria" (Memory) in 1999.

I will say only that in 1964 Sciascia wrote about the rediscovery of the cells and the visit we did together in a long note to the 1967 edition of *Morte dell'inquisitore* (*Death of the Inquisitor*), annotating generously: "It was right in those days when the work of restoration—and this time to restore the building to its original form—was going on, the journalist Giuseppe Quatriglio rediscovered three cells…"

The interview with Sciascia, published almost simultaneously by the *Giornale di Sicilia* of Palermo and the *Piccolo* of Trieste, a daily I collaborated with, was done in 1965. The interview, which has been quoted in the biographies of the writer, is interesting, I think, because in it he provided information on his literary enterprise that he never repeated.

We were in my house in my studio, sitting on the sofa. Sciascia did not seem to be in a hurry and seemed fairly relaxed and accessible.

On that occasion, he confided that he wrote his books and articles only in the morning hours. He never worked more than three consecutive hours and that he only wrote four pages, composing them directly on his portable typewriter. The afternoons—he added—he devoted to reading newspapers, new publications of old and often rare books dealing prevalently with Sicilian subjects that he had started to collect from antique book shops all over Italy. The following morning, he said, emphasizing the rigor of his method, he returned to his writing, but before reentering the interrupted text, he rewrote the last page of the day before in its entirety, convinced that the page finished when fatigue was setting in was probably more likely in need of revision.

From that time onward, I saw Sciascia very often as he had finally moved to Palermo. In the seventies, he frequently traveled to Rome, Milan, and especially Paris, often remaining there for two weeks sometimes. Sciascia's activities as a polemic writer continued. The major and best known national newspapers and magazines asked him to collaborate. Many of his novels are in my library with affectionate dedications neatly written with a fountain pen.

As I lived near his home, many times I went there early in the morning without announcing myself. Both he and his wife had authorized my unannounced incursion into their home. It was a simple ritual. I simply told the doorman to announce me and proceeded up to the apartment using the elevator. Often Leonardo came to the door, but sometimes it was his wife Maria who then introduced me to his studio, asking me to wait for the coffee. Leonardo would then chat with me for a while.

Sometimes, I would have to wait a bit before he came into the studio. I understood if he had work to do or if he wanted me to entertain him. Sometimes, I noticed that the sheet of paper in the typewriter was only half completed and in this case I would shorten my stay. At other times, Leonardo asked me to wait for him because he wanted to go out.

When he was working with the publisher Elvira Sellerio, he asked me to drive him to the publishing house. I did that gladly because being with Sciascia was always an enrichment. He always had some first hand interesting news to reveal, be it an advance notice of a publication or something else. It could take the form of sharing a confidence with his friend.

I recall the day when he told me with a satisfied air that he had completed his reading of the six volumes—thousands of pages—of the life of Giacomo Casanova. I recall that he spoke to me about his intentions of writing *Candido*, overcoming his initial perplexity about it. I recall his enthusiasm every time he found a Liberty object in the shops of antique dealers, or a walking cane with a silver handle, or an antique print that had a special significance for him.

His was a lesson for living and for writing. He had a great capacity for running through the events of the island and choosing some emblematic episodes that he would re-elaborate in his writing. To Sciascia as a teacher and a friend, I dedicated a book of short stories gathered from historical events buried in the archives. I considered my initiative a well earned homage to him. (*The Clock-Man and Other Stories*, Sellerio 1995.)

At the beginning of the eighties, when he was elected Deputy in the Italian Parliament, I met with him in Rome and I walked into the old restored building in the center of Rome that housed the offices of the members of Parliament. I saw him in his hotel or at a restaurant or coffee shop. In 1982, I was close to him during the writing of the minority report on the Moro case, a painful event that had appalled, moved, and shaken him for a long time. I was able to report in a published interview his extremely lucid analysis of the case.

Today, retracing in my memory the many meetings that passing of time distances ever farther, recalling all the articles I wrote on his books even in the *Giorno* of Milan and *El Pais* of Madrid, the interviews and the conversations we had, I hear the words of this great storyteller whose linguistic precision was proportional to the length of his silence. Sciascia spoke little, but he listened carefully and when he took part in the conversation he was essential, cutting, sometimes even ironic.

Today we continue to reflect on his premature death, on his loss at a moment when the world has undergone great changes, from the collapse of the Berlin Wall to the collapse of ideologies, events that would have certainly intrigued his curiosity. His strong artistic personality and his intellectual commitment that accepted the definition as an "enlightened" person have not been forgotten. He considered himself enlightened in the clarity of his language and ideas. There was then the problem of justice that in Sciascia was linked to the general problem of power and the inquisitorial power in its relationship with society. The theme of justice emerged powerfully, like a nagging thought that could not be suppressed. "The problem of the administration of justice—he stated in the eighties—has always been difficult, but I believe that the level of confusion that exists in Italy has not been reached by any civil society and no other democratic system of government."

Sciascia was a reticent man who never drove an automobile and never used a computer, but he knew how to read the signs of the times. His prestige was derived from this quality, but also from his fame as a "prophet," that often occasioned partisan accusations.

A heretic, an anti-conformist, a frontier's writer, Leonardo Sciascia appears as the writer of the second half of the twentieth century who was capable of restoring the primacy of literature with his masterful writing and sense of justice.

Rigor and morality, lacking his authoritative voice, are values that have disappeared from society and literature. There is a leveling, a reliance on conformism, the triumph of the philosophy of living for the day, which in the year 2000, seems depressing and without exit.

It's like remaining stuck in the mud without the strength or the ability to get up again.